Aztec Mythology

Captivating Aztec Myths of Gods, Goddesses,
and Legendary Creatures

Free Bonus from Captivating History (Available for a Limited time)

Hi History Lovers!

Now you have a chance to join our exclusive history list so you can get your first history ebook for free as well as discounts and a potential to get more history books for free! Simply visit the link below to join.

Captivatinghistory.com/ebook

Also, make sure to follow us on:

Twitter: @Captivhistory

Facebook: Captivating History

Youtube: Captivating History

Contents

Introduction

Between the ninth and the late eleventh centuries, a great migration began where tribes, including one who called themselves "Mexica," moved from places "far to the north" into what is now Central Mexico. The myths that describe this migration call the place of origin "Aztlan," which is sometimes translated as "Place of the White Heron," and it is from this name that we get the word "Aztecs," or "People from Aztlan."

The Aztec civilization of Central Mexico was not a single unitary culture but was rather made up of different peoples who spoke the Nahuatl language and who traced their origins to that far-off northern home. Over the centuries that followed the start of the migration from Aztlan, Aztec peoples established city-states and empires in Central Mexico, the largest of which was centered in the great city of Tenochtitlan, the capital of Mexica culture and political power, which had been built on the waters of Lake Texcoco. Today, that ancient capital has been overbuilt by Mexico City, the lake bed long ago having been drained of water.

By the time the Spanish arrived in 1519, the Aztec Empire was well established and had been consolidated under the umbrella of the Triple Alliance since 1428. This alliance of city-states included Mexico-Tenochtitlan, centered in the city of Tenochtitlan; the city-state of Texcoco, based on the eastern shore of the lake; and Tlacopan, a city-state on the western shore. The empire was orderly and prosperous; indeed, Spanish witnesses from the time of the conquest describe cities and markets that were larger, better built, and better organized than anything they had seen before. But only two years later, through a combination of war, conquest, and disease, the Aztec Empire was no more, and Mesoamerican culture and religion had been irrevocably damaged by the imposition of Spanish rule and the forced introduction of Christianity.

One of the primary difficulties in reconstructing the original mythological traditions of the Aztecs is the paucity of sources. In an act of iconoclasm born of efforts at Christianization, Spanish missionaries and government officials tracked down and burned Aztec books and government records. Of the many thousands of books and documents that must have once existed, only twelve are left today. Further, much else of what we know of Aztec myth and culture comes through the filter of early modern Spanish witnesses, whose cultural and religious biases undoubtedly skew much of what they reported.

However, invaders from across the sea were not the only iconoclasts: the Mexica emperor Itzcoatl (r. 1427 or 1428 to 1440 AD) consolidated his own power in part by revising history and myth in order to bolster claims of Mexica ascendancy in the region. Itzcoatl ordered the destruction of earlier codices and the creation of new ones that emphasized the legitimacy both of Mexica power and the supremacy of the Mexica war god Huitzilopochtli.

As a result of these instances of destruction, we therefore have only a partial view of what must have been the original Aztec mythos. However, what does exist shows a rich and complex tradition of origin myths, trickster tales, and mythologized pseudo-history that gives us a glimpse into the cosmology, religion, and world-view of this once-vibrant Mesoamerican culture.

2

The present book is divided into two sections. The first contains myths of the gods and goddesses, including the "Legend of the Suns," which is a complex of origin myths describing the creation of the world, followed by a tale that explains the origins of the Aztec practices of blood offerings and ritual warfare. Three other myths in this section relate the advent of other things important to Aztec life and culture: maize, pulque (an alcoholic beverage made from the sap of the maguey cactus), and music. A final story describes the Aztec concept of the afterlife.

The second section of the book contains Aztec political myths, all of which were intended to paint the Aztecs as a heroic people favored by the gods and worthy of conquering the civilizations they encountered. The first of these tales is the myth describing the Mexica journey from Aztlan to Central Mexico and the founding of the city of Tenochtitlan, all under the aegis of the god Huitzilopochtli. The second involves a mythical embassy to Aztlan commanded by the emperor Motecuhzoma I, who wishes to reconnect with the ancestral people there and with the mother of Huitzilopochtli, to let them know how great the Aztec Empire has become.

The remaining political stories in this section are a complex that create a mythical pseudo-history of the downfall of the Toltecs. Toltec civilization flourished in Central Mexico between the early tenth and late twelfth centuries and was one of the cultures that was displaced by the arrival of the Mexica and the imposition of Aztec rule in that region. In the third and fourth stories in this section, Huemac, the legendary last king of the Toltecs, is subjected to various misadventures and humiliations at the hands of Tezcatlipoca, the Aztec god of night, enmity, and discord, who presents himself in various disguises in order to play tricks on the king and destroy the Toltec people, while Huemac's own insolence towards the servants of Tlaloc, the god of rain, brings drought, famine, and a final prophecy of the end of Toltec culture.

One practice of the Toltec kings, who also functioned as priests in Toltec religion, was to claim the title of "Quetzalcoatl." In the final legend presented here, the priest-king is the god himself. Once again, Tezcatlipoca works his cunning against the Toltec ruler, this time turning him out of the city once and for all. The myth of how Quetzalcoatl exiled himself in shame from the Toltec capital, Tula, and then was transformed into the Morning Star is an episodic tale along the lines of the classic hero's journey.

In many of these myths, we see repeatedly the Aztec belief that offerings of human blood and human lives were necessary to the continued running of the universe. Indeed, in these myths the gods themselves make sacrifices of their own blood and even of their entire bodies in order to create a universe humans can live in and, in one story, to create humans themselves; humans therefore must make blood sacrifices in turn to feed the gods and to keep the universe in existence. To the ancient Aztecs, these practices seemed fitting, necessary, and honorable, helping to connect the world of humans to the divine world of the gods, a universe that in Aztec myth took shape in cycles of creation, destruction, and rebirth.

Note on the Aztec Calendar

A prominent feature of many ancient Mesoamerican civilizations is the use of well-constructed calendars and timekeeping systems. The Aztecs used two separate but interlocking yearly calendars: one was a 360-day solar year calendar, the other a 260-day ritual calendar. In addition, the Aztecs kept careful track of much longer spans of time, in particular the 52-year *xiuhmolpilli* (Bundle of Years) cycle.

The solar year was called "xihuitl" in Nahuatl, while the calendar for that year was known as *xiuhpohualli* (year count). This calendar was composed of eighteen months having twenty days each, for a total of 360 days. Each month was named after a specific religious festival, and days in this calendar were designated in much the same way as in the modern Western calendar. So, for example, days in the month called "Teotleco" (Return of the Gods) would be designated 1 Teotleco, 2 Teotleco, 3 Teotleco, and so on until 20 Teotleco was reached, at which point the new month would begin.

Because this 18-month calendar did not completely match the actual solar year, an additional five intercalary days were added at the end of the eighteenth month in order to keep the calendar aligned with the seasons. These five days were called "nemontemi" (nameless) and were considered to be very unlucky. The Aztecs were aware that the solar year is actually 365.25 days, but we do not know how they might have adjusted their calendars in order to account for the extra partial days.

The ritual calendar was called *tonalpohualli*, which means "count of day signs." The tonalpohualli was used to determine when specific rituals ought to be performed, as well as for astrology and auspice-taking, and was further connected to the world of the divine by having various gods preside over certain units of time as well as over specific days.

The Aztec sacred calendar was composed of a set of 20 "day signs," such as "Alligator," "Death," or "Flint Knife," that occurred and repeated in a fixed order. Alongside these signs was a count of 13 days that is known in Spanish as a *trecena* (the original Nahuatl word is unknown), such that a particular day could be called "3 Monkey" or "11 Reed," for example. The number count would restart when the thirteenth day was reached and continue numerically when the 20-day count ran out. Thus, the day-sign "Calli" (House) might be "1 Calli" in one cycle, but "8 Calli" in another. The table below shows all the day signs and the way they interact with the 13-day number count:

Day Name	Translation	Day Counts		
Cipactli	Alligator	1	8	2
Ehecatl	Wind	2	9	3
Calli	House	3	10	4
Cuetzpallin	Lizard	4	11	5
Coatl	Snake	5	12	6
Miquiztli	Death	6	13	7
Mazatl	Deer	7	1	8
Tochtli	Rabbit	8	2	9
Atl	Water	9	3	10
Itzcuintli	Dog	10	4	11
Ozomatli	Monkey	11	5	12
Malinalli	Grass	12	6	13
Acatl	Reed	13	7	1
Ocelotl	Jaguar	1	8	2
Cuauhtli	Eagle	2	9	3
Cozcacuauhtli	Vulture	3	10	4
Ollin	Movement	4	11	5

Tecpatl	Flint Knife	5	12	6
Quiahuitl	Rain	6	13	7
Xochitl	Flower	7	1	8 etc.

After Michael E. Smith, The Aztecs, 3rd ed. (Chicester: Wiley-Blackwell, 2011), 252.

As we see in the table, when a trecena runs out, a new one starts again with the next day sign. So, a trecena that starts on 1 Cipactli ends on 13 Acatl, and the new trecena begins on 1 Ocelotl and continues to the end of the day-sign list on 7 Xochitl. The day-sign list then restarts in the middle of the trecena, on 8 Calli, and this second trecena ends on 13 Miquiztli. The next trecena then starts on 1 Mazatl, and so on. This interlocking combination of 20 day signs and 13 numbers means that it takes 260 days to run through a complete cycle, which contains 260 unique combinations of day signs and numbers. Additionally, each trecena in the cycle was associated with a particular deity.

The solar calendar and ritual calendar when combined form a cycle that begins and ends in a space of 52 years. This cycle is known as *xiuhmolpilli* (Bundle of Years) in Nahuatl, although English-speaking scholars sometimes refer to it as the "calendar round." Similar to the ritual calendar, the count of the calendar round was based on the number 13, working within a cycle of 13 years, except with only four year signs instead of 20 day signs. These four years were called, in order, Tochtli, Acatl, Tecpatl, and Calli. Therefore, the year-cycle went 1 Tochtli, 2 Acatl, 3 Tecpatl, 4 Calli, 5 Tochtli, 6 Acatl, and so on until 13 years had passed and the next cycle would start on 1 Acatl. After 52 years, the cycle would return to its starting place on 1 Tochtli.

Within this cycle, days are described by their position in the solar calendar, the ritual calendar, and the four-name, 13-year cycle of counts within the calendar round. Because each day designation recurs every 52 years, Western scholars must make some calculations and research events in order to align the Aztec calendar to the Western one. If we take as our example the date of the arrival of the Spanish in Tenochtitlan, 8 November 1519, we would see that the designation for that day in the ritual calendar would be 8 Ehecatl; in the solar calendar it was 9 Quecholli; and the year was 1 Acatl. (Note: some alignments of the Western and Aztec calendars place this as 7 Cipactli, 8 Quecholli, 1 Acatl.)

We therefore see that the number 52 and its factors 4, 13, and 26 were central to the Aztec concept of time and practice of timekeeping, and that the 52-year xiuhmolpilli cycle was central to Aztec cosmology, since 52 was a number associated with completion and fullness of time. Every 52 years, the Aztecs celebrated the New Fire Ceremony, the successful performance of which they believed to be necessary to the continuation of the universe. The ceremony involved extinguishing all fires in the city, after which a man would be sacrificed by having his heart torn out; in his chest cavity, the new fire would be kindled. From this new flame, fires would be lit first in the temples, then in other important spaces, and then distributed to private homes. If the ceremony was not properly carried out, or if the fire failed to kindle, then the "tzitzimime," the spirits of the stars, would come to earth and devour the people. For the Aztecs, therefore, proper timekeeping and proper use of the calendar were more than just a way to keep track of days and years; it was a means by which to time the cycles of the universe itself, which human beings were responsible for keeping in motion through blood sacrifice.

PART I: AZTEC GODS, GODDESSES, AND COSMOLOGY

The Legend of the Suns

There is no unitary Aztec creation myth, but rather several variant tales of how the world came to be. One of the primary myths is the "Legend of the Suns," which explains the repeated creation, destruction, and recreation of the world until finally it assumes the form that we know it as today. These myths also explain why blood sacrifice was such an integral part of Aztec religious practice; it was this blood that kept the earth and the sun in existence because the gods who were the earth and sun demanded sustenance in that form.

We see here important connections between the Aztec concept of time as it was laid out in their calendrical system and their understanding of the phases of creation. Within Aztec culture and timekeeping practices, the number 13 was sacred and taken to represent a form of completeness, as was the number 52. Therefore, the first two "suns" represent a full and complete space of time, since their spans of 676 years are equal to 13 times 52. The second two "suns," however, are not full and complete in and of themselves, since they represent 7 times 52 and 6 times 52, respectively.

The number 4 likewise had associations with completeness through its function within the Aztec year count and in its reference to the four cardinal directions. We see these connections play out in the creation myth retold below with regard to the number of the first major gods created by the union of Tonacatecuhtli and Tonacacihuatl, the male and female aspects of the creator-god Ometeotl.

Long, long ago, before even time had come to be, there was Ometeotl, the Dual God. Ometeotl was made by the union of the god Tonacatecuhtli and the goddess Tonacacihuatl, the Lord and Lady of Our Sustenance. And so Ometeotl was both one and two at the same time. They came to be out of nothing, and for a time they were all that was in the whole of the universe, for nothing else had yet been made.

Tonacatecuhtli and Tonacacihuatl had four children. There was red Xipe Totec (the Flayed God), god of the seasons and the things that grow upon the earth; black Tezcatlipoca (Smoking Mirror), god of the earth; white Quetzalcoatl (Plumed Serpent), god of air; and blue Huitzilopochtli (Hummingbird of the South), god of war. The god-children lived in the thirteenth heaven with their parents. Of these children, Tezcatlipoca was the most powerful. Together the four children of the Dual God decided that they would like to create a world and some people to live in it. It took them several tries before the world became the way we know it today because the gods fought over who should be the sun and rule the earth.

The first attempt at creation was made by Quetzalcoatl and Huitzilopochtli. First, they made a fire, which was the sun. But it wasn't big or strong enough to give much light or heat, as it was only half of a sun.

After they made the sun, Quetzalcoatl and Huitzilopochtli made a man and a woman. They called the woman Oxomoco, and the man Cipactonal. The gods told the man and the woman what work they were to do. The man was to be a farmer, while the woman's duty was to spin thread and weave cloth. The gods gave the woman the gift of maize. Some of the grains were magical and could cure illnesses or help foretell the future. Together Oxomoco and Cipactonal had many children, who became the macehuales, the farmers who worked the land.

Even though there was already a half-sun, and even though there were already a man and a woman, the gods had not yet created time. This they did by making days and months. Each month had twenty-one days. And when eighteen months had gone by, this made three hundred and sixty days, and that span the gods called a year.

After there was a sun, a man and a woman, and time, the gods created the underworld, which was called Mictlan. Then Quetzalcoatl and Huitzilopochtli made two other gods to rule over this place. They were called Mictlantecuhtli and Mictecacihuatl, the Lord and Lady of Mictlan.

When all this was done, Quetzalcoatl and Huitzilopochtli created some water, and in it they placed a giant fish. The fish was called Cipactli, and the earth was made out of the body of the fish.

Oxomoco and Cipactonal had a son named Piltzintecuhtli. The gods looked upon him and saw that he had no wife. At that time, there was a goddess of beauty and young women called Xochiquetzal (Flower Quetzal Feather). The gods took some of Xochiquetzal's hair and from it they made a woman to be Piltzintecuhtli's wife.

The gods looked at all the things they had created, and they were not satisfied with them, especially with the sun, which was too weak to give much light. Tezcatlipoca thought about how to make the old sun brighter, but then he thought of a better idea: he turned himself into the sun. This new sun was much better than the old one. It was a whole sun, and it gave enough light to the world the gods had made. This was the beginning of the first age of the world, the age of the First Sun.

The gods also wanted more beings in their new world. They made a race of giants who ate nothing but pine nuts. The giants were very

11

large and very strong. So strong were these giants that they could uproot trees with their bare hands.

So, for a time, Tezcatlipoca shone brightly over the world the gods had made. But after this world had existed for 13 times 52 years, or 676 years, Quetzalcoatl thought his brother had reigned as the sun for long enough. He took his club and struck Tezcatlipoca with it, sending him plummeting down, down, down into the waters that encircled the world. Tezcatlipoca was very angry that Quetzalcoatl had done this. He rose up out of the water in the shape of a giant jaguar, and in this shape, he roamed about the whole earth. The jaguar hunted all the giants and devoured every one of them. Once all the giants had been eaten, Tezcatlipoca rose back up into the heavens, where he became the constellation Jaguar (Ursa Major).

The second age of the world was the age of the Second Sun. This was the age of wind. Quetzalcoatl made this world, and Quetzalcoatl was the sun during this age. The macehuales lived in this age eating nothing but pine nuts. The second age also lasted for 676 years, until Tezcatlipoca took his revenge on his brother. Tezcatlipoca came to the world in a blast of wind so great that Quetzalcoatl and the macehuales were blown away, although some of the macehuales escaped the blast. These turned into monkeys, and they ran away into the jungles to live.

After the time of the Second Sun was complete, the god of rain whose name was Tlaloc (He Who Makes Things Sprout) became the sun and ruler of creation, and his age is the age of the Third Sun. This age lasted for seven times 52 years, or 364 years. During this age, the people ate the seeds of a plant that grew in the water. But again, Quetzalcoatl destroyed this world. He brought down a rain made of fire, and all the people were turned into birds.

After Quetzalcoatl ended the reign of Tlaloc, he gave the world to Tlaloc's wife, Chalchiuhtlicue (Jade Skirt Woman) to rule. Chalchiuhtlicue was the goddess of rivers, streams, and all manner of waters. She was the sun for six times 52 years, or 312 years. This

Fourth Sun age was a time of great rain. It rained so long and so hard that there was a great flood that covered the earth. The flood washed away the macehuales, turning them into fish. After the flood was over, the sky fell down and covered the earth so that nothing could live on it.

The gods looked upon the world they had made and saw how it had been destroyed by their quarreling. Quetzalcoatl and Tezcatlipoca made peace with one another and went down to rebuild the world. The gods each went to one end of the world, where they transformed themselves into great trees. With their mighty tree-limbs, they pushed the sky back up into its place, and they hold it there still.

The god Tonacatecuhtli, father of Quetzalcoatl and Tezcatlipoca, looked down and saw that the brothers had ceased their fighting and had worked together to mend what their anger had broken. Tonacatecuhtli therefore gave the brothers the starry heavens to rule, and he made a highway of stars for them to use as they traveled; this highway is the Milky Way.

Then the gods created new people to walk upon the earth. Once the sky had been put back in its place, Tezcatlipoca took flint and used it to make fires. These fires lit the world, for the old sun had been destroyed in the flood and a new one had not yet been made. Also, there were no people, for the giants had all been devoured, and the people had all been turned into monkeys, birds, and fish. So, Tezcatlipoca met with his brothers to take counsel about what to do. Together they decided that a new sun would have to be created, but this would be a new kind of sun, one that ate human hearts and drank human blood. Without sacrifices to feed it, this sun would cease to shine, and the world would return to darkness once more. So, the gods made four hundred men and five women, and these were to be food for the new sun.

Some say that Quetzalcoatl and Tlaloc each wanted their sons to become the Fifth Sun, and that these gods each took their sons to one of the great fires that had been kindled. Quetzalcoatl's son had been born without a mother. The god threw his son into the fire first, and he became the new sun. His son rose out of the fire and went into the sky where he still is to this day. Tlaloc waited until the fire had nearly burned itself out. He took his son, whose mother was Chalchiuhtlicue, and threw him into the glowing embers and ashes. Tlaloc's son rose out of the fire and went into the sky as the moon. Because Quetzalcoatl's son went into the blazing fire, he became a creature of fire and glows with a light that is too bright to look at. But because Tlaloc's son went into the embers and ashes, his light is dimmer and his face is splattered with ashes. And this is how night became divided from day, and why the moon and the sun cross the sky in different ways and along different paths.

But another tale tells how the sickly god Nanahuatzin willingly sacrificed himself to become the Fifth Sun. The gods had gathered at the great city of Teotihuacan to discuss how they might make a new sun to replace the old one that had been destroyed in the flood. One of them needed to jump into a bright bonfire and then rise into the sky. Nanahuatzin, god of disease, whose name means "Full of Sores," came forward. "I will do this thing," he said, "even though my body is diseased and bent, and even though my skin is covered with leprosy."

The other gods laughed at Nanahuatzin. They said, "You silly fellow. You are sickly and weak. You will not have the courage to jump into the fire. Let someone else become the sun."

Then Tecuciztecatl (The One from the Place of the Conch), came forward. He was a most wealthy god, well made in his body and well dressed with all manner of gold and feather ornaments. "I will do this thing," he said, "for it would be better that a healthy god make this sacrifice than a sickly one."

The other gods agreed that it should be so and caused a great fire to be kindled. While this was being done, Tecuciztecatl and Nanahuatzin retired to places where they might fast and prepare offerings to purify themselves so that they would be worthy to

14

become the new sun. Tecuciztecatl prepared offerings that were made of the finest things, of jade and quetzal feathers, and balls of gold. Nanahuatzin's offerings were humble reeds and the spines of the maguey cactus.

At the appointed time, Tecuciztecatl and the other gods gathered around the fire. The wealthy god, dressed in his best finery, strode up to the great blaze with its searing heat. He made as though to throw himself in, but at the last minute he balked and walked away. Again, he tried, but he could not bring himself to jump into the flames. He tried again, and yet again, but each time his courage failed him. After the fourth time, he walked away from the bonfire and from the other gods, ashamed that he had not been able to turn himself into the sun as he had boasted he would do.

The other gods wondered how they would make a new sun, since Tecuciztecatl had failed to jump into the fire. But all was not lost; Nanahuatzin had not forgotten his offer to become the new sun, and he had also fasted and purified himself so that he might be a fitting sacrifice. The sickly god stepped forward, dressed in garments made of paper, and walked straight up to the raging fire. He stared into the heart of the blaze for just a moment, then threw himself into the very heart of the flames.

Nanahuatzin's hair was ablaze. His clothing was ablaze. His skin crackled with the heat of the flames that licked all around his body. Tecuciztecatl saw the courage of the sickly Nanahuatzin and was deeply ashamed. So, he also stepped forward and jumped into the flames with Nanahuatzin. An eagle and a jaguar had been watching the sacrifice too. They saw the courage of Nanahuatzin and of Tecuciztecatl, and so they joined the gods, throwing themselves among the flames. This is why the eagle's feathers are tipped with black, and why the jaguar is covered with black spots. This is also why the Aztecs created the orders of the eagle and the jaguar to honor their bravest warriors.

After the eagle and jaguar had thrown themselves into the fire, the other gods waited to see what would become of Nanahuatzin and Tecuciztecatl. Slowly, slowly, light began to rim the world. The gods looked all around, wondering where the source of the light was. Then suddenly Nanahuatzin burst forth over the eastern horizon, covering the world with the brightest light. His sacrifice transformed him from the lowly, sickly leper-god into a new sun-god: Ollin Tonatiuh, whose name means "Movement of the Sun."

But Tecuciztecatl also had been transformed by his sacrifice, and shortly after Nanahuatzin rose into the sky, so did Tecuciztecatl. And now the gods had a new problem, for there was not one but two suns in the sky, and the light they made together was too bright for anyone to see anything. One of the gods snatched up a rabbit that was nearby and flung it into the face of Tecuciztecatl. The rabbit hit Tecuciztecatl so hard that his light was dimmed. That was how the moon was created, and the shape of a rabbit was now permanently marked on his face.

Then the gods rejoiced for now they had both a sun and a moon. But their joy was short-lived for Tonatiuh refused to move from his place in the sky until all the gods had sacrificed themselves to him. The other gods grew angry and refused to do this thing, but Tonatiuh was steadfast. He would not move until he had drunk the blood of the other gods.

Tlahuizcalpantecuhtli (Lord of Dawn), who is the Morning Star, said, "I will stop Tonatiuh. I will save you from having to be sacrificed." Tlahuizcalpantecuhtli threw a dart at Tonatiuh with all his might, but it missed. Tonatiuh threw a dart of his own back at the Morning Star, hitting him in the head. This changed Tlahuizcalpantecuhtli into Itztlacoliuhqui (Curved Obsidian), the god of coldness, frost, and obsidian, and this is why it is always cold right before the sun rises.

The other gods realized they could no longer refuse what Tonatiuh demanded. They came before him with bare breasts, and

Quetzalcoatl cut out their hearts with a sacrificial knife. Once the gods had been sacrificed, Quetzalcoatl took their clothing and ornaments and wrapped them into sacrificial bundles. These sacred bundles were then worshipped by the people.

Sated with the blood of the gods, Tonatiuh began to move across the sky, and he has done so ever since. And this was the birth of the Fifth Sun, the Sun under which all life lives to this day. But still the people offer blood and hearts to the sun, to ensure that he is satisfied and to keep him on his sacred path across the sky.

Now, another legend says that the remaking of the earth after the great flood happened in a different way. This tale says that Quetzalcoatl and Tezcatlipoca looked down and saw that there was nothing but water, but in this water swam a great monster. The monster's name was Tlaltecuhtli, which means "Earth Lord," even though the creature itself was female. It was a giant thing, with mouths all over its body and a ravenous desire to eat flesh. The gods thought it likely that the monster would devour anything they managed to create, so they devised a plan to be rid of Tlaltecuhtli and make a new earth at the same time. Quetzalcoatl and Tezcatlipoca therefore transformed themselves into monstrous serpents. In these forms, they dove into the water and attacked Tlaltecuhtli. The gods wrapped themselves around the body of the monster and began to pull. No matter how hard Tlaltecuhtli thrashed, she could not escape the grip of the gods. Slowly, the body of the monster began to tear apart, until finally it was torn in two. The top half of Tlaltecuhtli became the new earth, and the bottom half was flung up into the sky to become the heavens.

Tlaltecuhtli screamed in pain as she was torn asunder. The other gods heard her in her agony and were angry at what Quetzalcoatl and Tezcatlipoca had done to her, but they could not heal her wounds. Instead, they transformed her body. Her hair became flowers, shrubs, and trees, and from her skin grew the grasses. Fresh water sprang from her eyes in the form of rivers, wells, and streams, and her mouths became the caves of the world. Mountains and valleys were

17

made from her nose. But even though she was no longer a monster, Tlaltecuhtli still had a need for fresh blood and flesh, and so once the people had been created, they made sacrifices to feed her. In this way, the earth continues to provide all the things that people and animals need to live.

But the gods first needed to create the new people since all the people who had lived under the previous four Suns had been turned into monkeys, birds, and fish, and that the bones of those who had died were kept in Mictlan. So, the gods sent Quetzalcoatl to Mictlan to see whether he might fetch the bones of the ones who had been turned into fish.

"O Mictlantecuhtli," said Quetzalcoatl, "I have come seeking the bones of the people who were turned into fish."

"Why do you want them?" asked the Lord of Mictlan.

"The earth was destroyed in the great flood," said Quetzalcoatl, the Plumed Serpent, "and we have rebuilt it and made a new sun and moon and a new sky, but there are no people. We wish to use the bones to make new people, for it is good that the earth be inhabited."

But Mictlantecuhtli was jealous of all the things that he kept within his realm. He did not care whether the earth had people on it or not, and he did not want Quetzalcoatl to have the bones. So, he gave Quetzalcoatl a test.

Mictlantecuhtli handed a conch shell to Quetzalcoatl and said, "You may have the bones if you walk four times around all of Mictlan while blowing blasts on this conch shell."

Quetzalcoatl thought that this was an easy challenge to pass, until he looked closely at the shell. It had not yet been made into a trumpet, and there was no way for him to make any sounds on it. But Quetzalcoatl was friends with the worms. He called the worms to come and make holes in the shell. Quetzalcoatl also was friends with the bees. He called the bees to come and buzz inside the shell to make a great noise. And so, Quetzalcoatl was able to pass the test that the Lord of Mictlan had set for him.

Mictlantecuhtli gave the bones to Quetzalcoatl, as he had promised, but he had no intention of allowing them to leave Mictlan. Mictlantecuhtli ordered his servants to dig a deep pit along the path that Quetzalcoatl was taking. Now, Quetzalcoatl knew that Mictlantecuhtli was not trustworthy, and so he was hurrying to leave Mictlan before the bones were taken away from him. As Quetzalcoatl ran along the path, Mictlantecuhtli sent a bird to fly in the Plumed Serpent's face and frighten him just as he approached the pit. When the bird flew at Quetzalcoatl, he lost his footing and tumbled down into the pit. His fall broke the fish bones into many pieces, and this is why people are of all different sizes.

After a time, Quetzalcoatl recovered from his fall. He gathered up all the pieces of the bones and climbed out of the pit. He was able to safely leave Mictlan, and by and by he came to a place called Tamoanchan, Land of the Misty Sky, a holy and blessed place. Quetzalcoatl gave the bones to the goddess Cihuacoatl, Woman Serpent. Cihuacoatl put the bones in her quern and ground them into a fine flour. She put the bone flour into a special jar, and all the gods gathered around it. One by one, the gods pierced their flesh and let drops of their blood drip onto the bones. When the bones and blood were all mixed into dough, the gods shaped it into the forms of people. The gods gave the dough forms life and put them upon the earth to live.

And these are the tales of how creation came to be, and why we live under the Fifth Sun, and why the earth and the sun demand sacrifices from the people who live upon the earth under the light of the sun.

The Deeds of Mixcoatl

One surviving original work by sixteenth-century Spanish friar Andrés de Olmos is the Historia de los Mexicanos por sus pinturas (History of the Mexicans as Told by Their Pictures). *In this work, which is also known as the* Codex Ramirez, *de Olmos gives accounts of Aztec myths. One section of the codex is devoted to the god Camaxtli, who was also known as Mixcoatl (Cloud Serpent). De Olmos understood Mixcoatl as an aspect of Tezcatlipoca rather than as a separate figure. In this brief tale, Mixcoatl, god of hunting and the Milky Way, is said to have originated both ritual warfare and the Aztec practice of piercing the tongue and ears to bring forth a blood offering.*

Ritual warfare was an important aspect of Aztec life. Sacrifices for the gods had to be acquired in some manner and in some quantity, so Aztec city-states would challenge one another to battles on a regular basis. The purpose of this warfare was not conquest, and neither was it the point to kill as many of the enemy as possible. Rather, the warriors were expected to capture as many of the enemy as they could. These captives were then brought back to the victors' home city where they became sacrificial victims. The Aztecs believed that the noblest deaths a man could hope for were either to perish in battle or to be offered in sacrifice to the gods, after which the soul would be transformed into a hummingbird.

The name "Chichimecs" referred to the various peoples who lived outside the Valley of Mexico and sometimes had connotations similar to that of our English word "barbarian." Here we see that Mixcoatl creates these people precisely so that they can be slaughtered, and he also turns them into drunkards, a state that was anathema to the Aztecs and could be punished by death.

And so, it came to pass that one year after the new sun had been created and fed by the blood of the gods that Mixcoatl thought to himself that it would be a good thing to ensure that the sun never lacked for blood or hearts. Therefore, he went up into the eighth heaven and there he made four men and a woman.

"Go down to earth," said Mixcoatl to the new people. "Go there and learn the art of war, for the sun has need of blood to drink and hearts to eat."

Mixcoatl then cast the new people down to the earth, where they landed in the water. But they immediately returned to the heavens, and so Mixcoatl's wish that they should make war did not come to pass. So, the next year Mixcoatl again bethought himself how to create new people so that there could be war and sacrifices, and this time he went to the earth and found a great stone, which he struck heavily with his club. The stone split open, and from it came forth 400 Chichimecs, who were the first people to live in Mexico before the Aztecs came.

Mixcoatl saw that his efforts had thus far come to naught because the Chichimecs did not yet know the art of war for they had no enemies, and they did not make war amongst themselves since they were kin to one another, and the original five people he had created to make war to provide blood and hearts to the sun had returned to the heavens. So, for eleven years Mixcoatl did penance. He took the sharp spines of the maguey cactus, and with these, he pierced his tongue and his ears. He pierced them so that the blood dripped down as an offering and a penance, so that the four men and one woman he had created would come back to earth and make war upon the Chichimecs. And in this way Mixcoatl began the practice of these small blood offerings using the spines of the maguey on the tongue and ears, which the people then also did in reverence and supplication to the gods.

When Mixcoatl's penance was done, the four sons and one daughter he created came down from the heavens. They went to the earth, where they made homes in trees, and in the trees, they fed the eagles who also made their nests there.

Now, while the five first children of Mixcoatl were making their new homes in the trees, Mixcoatl bethought himself of ways to make the Chichimecs and his five children make war upon one another to provide blood and hearts for the sun. Therefore, Mixcoatl took the sap of the maguey and showed the Chichimecs how to make pulque and other wines from it. Once the Chichimecs learned how good this wine was, they spent all their time making it and drinking it, and thus spent their days in drunkenness. And so, it came to pass that one day the Chichimecs saw the five children of Mixcoatl where they sat in their trees, and the children saw that the Chichimecs were drunken and worthless. Therefore, the children came down from the trees and slew all the Chichimecs except for three who escaped, one of these being Mixcoatl, who had turned himself into a Chichimec.

And so, this was how Mixcoatl taught the people the art of warfare and the proper way to do penance, that there might always be blood and hearts with which to feed the sun.

The Origin of Maize and the Creation of Pulque

Two of the most important staples in Aztec agriculture were maize and maguey, which is a type of agave cactus. Maize was—and still is—a staple food for many Central American traditional cultures and had an important place in their mythology and their concepts of themselves as peoples. Pulque was an intoxicating beverage used primarily for ritual purposes, but the maguey plant had uses beyond providing the sap from which pulque was fermented. The leaves were edible and were used to make paper; the thorns were used as ritual objects and as needles; and rope and cloth could be made from its fibers. In the stories about maize and pulque, as in the above tale of the creation of new people from fish bones and gods' blood, we see the vital function of Quetzalcoatl as a trickster who uses his shapeshifting abilities to find things that will benefit human beings.

Oxomoco and Cipactonal, the first man and woman ever created, play a role in bringing maize to the people. Here we see that Aztec myth is divided as to which of these mythical personages is male and which female. In the "Legend of the Suns," told above, Oxomoco is female and Cipactonal male, but in the story of the origin of maize, these genders are reversed.

Once the gods had recreated people out of their own blood and the bones of the fish that Quetzalcoatl brought out of Mictlan, they saw that these new beings had no food to eat, so they went looking for a source of food for the people. Quetzalcoatl looked and looked, and finally he saw a little ant carrying a kernel of maize in its jaws.

"Where did you get that?" said Quetzalcoatl to the ant.

"I'm not going to tell you," said the ant, and it continued its march back to its hive.

Quetzalcoatl followed the ant. "That looks like a fine kind of food," said the god. "Where did you get it?"

But the ant wouldn't answer. It kept walking along with the maize in its jaws. Quetzalcoatl wouldn't give up. "Where did you get that?" he said to the ant.

The ant saw that the god would not leave it alone until it answered his question, so the ant took Quetzalcoatl to a great mountain called Tonacatepetl, the Mountain of Food. Quetzalcoatl saw long lines of ants streaming into and out of the mountain. He changed himself into an ant and followed his guide into the mountain. Inside the mountain were huge piles of maize and other good things to eat. Still in his ant-form, Quetzalcoatl picked up a kernel of maize in his jaws and brought it outside the mountain. When he had collected enough maize, he brought it back to Tamoanchan, the blessed place, where the gods were waiting with their newly-made people. Quetzalcoatl gave the grains of maize to the gods. They tasted the maize and realized that it would make the best food of all for the new people. But they did not know how to get it out of the mountain and carry it to their new people, for turning themselves into ants to remove it one kernel at a time would take too much time and labor.

"I know!" said Quetzalcoatl to the other gods. "I will go and get the mountain and bring it here, if you will help me."

So, the gods went to Mount Tonacatepetl together. They tied many strong ropes around the mountain. They pulled and pulled and pulled, but the mountain would not move. Quetzalcoatl and the other gods went back to Tamoanchan feeling very discouraged.

Then Oxomoco took some of the grains of maize that Quetzalcoatl had brought back with him. With the help of his wife, Cipactonal, Oxomoco performed a divination with the maize.

"What do the kernels of maize tell you?" asked Quetzalcoatl.

Oxomoco said, "The mountain must be broken open, but the only one who can do this thing is Nanahuatzin."

Nanahuatzin, the sickly god, agreed to open the Mountain of Food. He asked Tlaloc, the god of rain, whether he might have the help of the tlaloque, the servants of Tlaloc who are the lords of rain and lightning. Tlaloc said, "I will gladly let them go with you."

Tlaloc summoned his four servants, and these were the blue tlaloque, the white tlaloque, the yellow tlaloque, and the red tlaloque. "You will go with Nanahuatzin and help him break open the mountain of food," said Tlaloc to his servants.

And so Nanahuatzin and the tlaloque went to Mount Tonacatepetl. Nanahuatzin and the tlaloque used their powers to split the mountain open. Out of the mountain poured every good thing: maize, beans, amaranth, and many other seeds that the people could plant and eat for food. But the gods were jealous of this bounty, and so the tlaloque took it all away. Thus, it is that Tlaloc and his servants dole out rain and food to the people in season.

Quetzalcoatl and the other gods looked upon the people they had made. The people had food to eat and seeds to plant, and the land they lived in was good, but the people were not happy. So, Quetzalcoatl set out to find something that would help the new people have happiness as well as good food. The god went up into the heavens, where he found Mayahuel, the goddess of the maguey cactus. Mayahuel was the granddaughter of a tzitzimitl, which is a deity of a star that shines in the night sky. Quetzalcoatl went to Mayahuel and said, "Come with me to earth. I need your help to make a thing for the people so that they can be happy."

Mayahuel secretly went with Quetzalcoatl, for she feared the wrath of her grandmother and the other tzitzimime, who struggle every night to keep shining in the black sky but are pushed away by the sun. Together Mayahuel and Quetzalcoatl entwined their bodies, turning themselves into a tall tree. Mayahuel was one branch of the tree, and Quetzalcoatl was the other. When Mayahuel's grandmother woke from her sleep, she saw that her granddaughter was missing. She called to the tzitzimime and ordered them to find and kill Mayahuel.

The tzitzimime went down to Earth. They searched high and low for Mayahuel, until finally they came upon the tree that she and Quetzalcoatl had become. The tzitzimime attacked the tree. They knocked it down and broke the branches apart. Mayahuel's grandmother recognized the branch that was Mayahuel. She broke it into many small pieces and gave these to the other tzitzimime to eat.

Quetzalcoatl's branch was not touched by the tzitzimime, and when these star-gods had gone back to the heavens, Quetzalcoatl resumed his own form. He looked about him and saw the bones of Mayahuel scattered in pieces all around. Sorrowful, Quetzalcoatl picked up the bones. He planted them carefully in the earth, and after a time, maguey plants sprang from them. Quetzalcoatl then took the sap from the plants and fermented it into pulque. He brought the pulque to the people and gave it to them to drink. They found that when they drank it, their hearts were lighter, and it made them want to sing and dance.

And so, it was that the gods gave the people maize to be their food and pulque to be their wine.

How Quetzalcoatl Brought Music to the People

This story survives in three early modern sources, all of which originally were written in Spanish, and shows Quetzalcoatl operating in his secondary persona as Ehecatl, the wind-god. The names of Tezcatlipoca's servants are given here in only English because there is some confusion over the Nahuatl names given in the sources and what types of creatures are indicated.

The Spanish missionaries Juan de Torquemada, writing in the early seventeenth century, and Gerónimo de Mendieta, writing in the late sixteenth, list these servants as "ballena, sirena, y tortuga" (whale, mermaid, and turtle). Nahuatl names are preserved in the French version of a lost sixteenth-century treatise by Spanish missionary Andrés de Olmos. However, in his modern edition of the French translation of Olmos' treatise, Édouard de Jonghe suggests that the Nahuatl names would seem to list a mermaid (Aciuatl, literally, "fish woman"), a crocodile (Acipactli), and another creature the nature of which is uncertain. De Jonghe posits that the name for the third creature might originally have been compounded from the Nahuatl words for "reed" and "shell," but he suggests that transmission of this name appears to have been corrupt. Because of the difficulties with the original Nahuatl, I am giving English names only to these servants, while trying to hew as closely as possible to what is known of the Nahuatl originals based on de Jonghe's notes in his edition of Olmos' text.

The versions of this myth in the Spanish sources are rather laconic. Therefore, I have taken the liberty of fleshing the myth out somewhat to make it a better story.

There was a time when Quetzalcoatl tired of being the Plumed Serpent. He changed himself into Ehecatl, which means "Wind." Ehecatl flew up and down the land, blowing the clouds about. He made the treetops dance with the force of his breath. He went out to sea and made a huge storm that whirled and blew and stirred up waves as big as houses. Quetzalcoatl had a fine time being Wind.

While he was doing this, he happened to blow past his brother, Tezcatlipoca, the Smoking Mirror. "Stop blowing for a minute," said Tezcatlipoca. "I have something to ask you."

Ehecatl stood still and said, "Ask, brother."

26

"Have you looked upon these new people we have made? I think there might be something missing for them," said Tezcatlipoca.

"No, I have not looked upon them much lately," said Ehecatl, "for I have been Wind and have not stood still for long. But have they not good food to eat and cool water to drink? Have they not bright feathers and good woven cloth to adorn themselves? Have they not tools and skills with which to do their work? Do they not worship the gods as they ought? What could be missing for them?"

Tezcatlipoca thought for a minute. His brother had listed many good things the people had. But still there seemed to be something missing.

"I know!" said the Smoking Mirror. "I know what is missing. The people do not have music. We must find a way to give them music so that they might sing and dance, for those are joyful things that they do not have. And with songs and dances they can make their worship of the gods even better and more beautiful."

"That is a fine idea," said Ehecatl. "Let us give music to the people."

"Yes," said Tezcatlipoca, "but there is one problem. Music belongs to Tonatiuh, to the god of the Sun. Can you go up into the heavens and take it from him?"

"I think I can," said Ehecatl, "but I will need your help."

Tezcatlipoca agreed to help Ehecatl. First the two gods went to the shore of the sea together. There Tezcatlipoca called his servants, Crocodile Woman, Fish Woman, and Reed-and-Shell Woman and told them to give Ehecatl whatever aid he might need.

The first thing Ehecatl needed to do was to get up into the heavens where the Sun lived and kept his musicians. It was too high for Ehecatl to fly by himself. He needed a great bridge to get there. Ehecatl went to the servants of Tezcatlipoca and said, "Build me a bridge to the house of the Sun."

Crocodile Woman, Fish Woman, and Reed-and-Shell Woman worked together. Soon they had made a fine bridge that went all the way up to the house of the Sun. Ehecatl walked along the bridge. As he grew nearer to the house of the Sun, he began to hear the sounds of flutes, drums, and singing, but he could not yet see who was making these sounds. Closer and closer he came, and soon he could see the musicians. Some of them were wearing yellow clothing. Others wore white. And the rest were clad in blue or red.

But before Ehecatl could get close enough to speak to the musicians, Tonatiuh saw him approaching. "Why are you coming to my house, O Wind?" asked the sun-god.

"I am coming to find music and bring it to the people," said Ehecatl.

Tonatiuh did not want Ehecatl to take away his musicians. The Sun told the musicians to hide themselves and to be silent, so that Ehecatl would not be able to find them, but it was too late. Ehecatl had already heard them playing and singing. He had seen their bright clothing. Ehecatl knew that the musicians were there. He also knew that no musician could be silent for long. So, Ehecatl began to sing. "Come with me down to earth; play and sing for the people there," sang Ehecatl.

The musicians remained silent because they feared the wrath of the Sun. Tonatiuh was satisfied. He thought Ehecatl would never find his servants and that music would belong to him alone, forever. Ehecatl was not discouraged. He reached the end of the bridge and entered the house of the Sun. Ehecatl tried again, making his song even more beautiful than before. "Come with me down to earth; play and sing for the people there," sang the Wind.

But still the musicians were silent. Tonatiuh saw that Ehecatl had entered his house and was looking for the musicians. The Sun tried to stand in the way of the Wind, but the Wind was too quick for him. Ehecatl flew around Tonatiuh. He flew through all the chambers of the house of the Sun, singing, "Come with me down to earth; play and sing for the people there," and this time the musicians answered him. They played rhythms on their drums and tunes on their flutes, and sang back, "Take us to earth to play and to sing."

Still Tonatiuh tried to catch Ehecatl, but each time Ehecatl flew nimbly out of reach. Following the sound of drums and flutes, Ehecatl went to the chamber where the musicians were hiding. "Come with me," sang Ehecatl.

"Take us to earth," sang the musicians.

And so Ehecatl wrapped the musicians in his feathered cloak. He sped through the chambers and halls of the house of the Sun, bearing the musicians with him. Tonatiuh pursued Ehecatl with all the swiftness he had, but it was not enough to catch the Wind. Ehecatl carried the musicians down the bridge that the servants of Tezcatlipoca had made. When he neared the bottom, he cried out, "Crocodile Woman! Fish Woman! Reed-and-Shell Woman! Tear down the bridge so that the Sun may not follow!"

The servants of Tezcatlipoca did as Ehecatl commanded. They tore down the bridge, stranding Tonatiuh in the heavens. Ehecatl turned himself into a gentle breeze and floated down to earth with the musicians. When they reached the ground, Ehecatl unwound his cloak and set the musicians on the ground. "This is earth," said Ehecatl. "Go to the people and teach them your music."

The musicians went straight away to the nearest village. They showed the people how to make flutes and drums and how to make horns out of conch shells. They taught the people how to play those instruments and how to sing and make new songs. They went from village to village, teaching all they knew. And then the people taught their children, and their children's children, and soon every village throughout the world was full of the sounds of flutes, drums, and singing.

And that is how the Plumed Serpent brought music to the people.

The Fall of Xochiquetzal

Xochiquetzal was a goddess of craftspeople, especially weavers and workers in precious metals. She also was a goddess of fertility, childbirth, and female sexual power, and as such was particularly associated with female beauty and with flowers. This story of her exile from the paradise of Tamoanchan has parallels with the Genesis story of Adam and Eve.

As in the biblical story of Eve and the apple, Xochiquetzal's sin involves the violation of a rule given by a supreme deity—in this case, the creator-god Ometeotl—about a sacred tree. While Aztec codices also contain representations of sacred trees, the concept of a Great Tree or World Tree may originally have been taken from the Mayans, as was the Aztec name for the paradise of the gods; "Tamoanchan" is a Mayan word, not an Aztec one.

Long, long ago, there was a place called Tamoanchan. Tamoanchan was a place of plenty, where it was always sweet summer, and the birds sang in the boughs of the trees. It was in Tamoanchan the gods and goddesses made their home.

In the center of Tamoanchan was a great tree. It had a thick trunk covered with smooth bark. It had branches reaching up to the sky, covered with green leaves and beautiful flowers and bright fruit. The tree had been planted there by Ometeotl themselves, and they told the other gods and goddesses that no one was to touch the tree or pick its flowers or fruit. And for a long time, the gods and goddesses obeyed what Ometeotl commanded.

Among the gods and goddesses who lived in Tamoanchan was Xochiquetzal (Flower Quetzal Feather). She was the most beautiful of all the goddesses and was attended at all times by entertainers who danced and sang for her. Xochiquetzal loved beautiful things and could make them with her own hands. She especially loved weaving, for in a piece of cloth she could weave all the colors of the world.

Xochiquetzal also loved the Great Tree of Ometeotl. She loved the green of its leaves, the colors of its flowers, and the scent of its bright fruit. But most of all, she loved to sit in the shade of the tree while she did her work, and while her entertainers danced and sang for her. Day after day, she gazed at the colors and smelled the scents of the Great Tree, and day after day she felt more and more tempted to pick some of these for herself.

Finally, Xochiquetzal could stand the temptation no more. "The tree has many flowers," she said to herself, "and it bears a great deal of fruit. Surely if I pick only one or two of these it will do no harm."

And so, she picked two flowers to put into her hair and one piece of fruit to eat. No sooner had Xochiquetzal plucked these things than the tree began to sway as though in a strong wind. Its branches creaked and groaned. The leaves came cascading down as though it were autumn. And then with a great *crack* the tree split open. The pieces fell to the ground, and when it struck the earth, the branches all shattered and were strewn about like so much matchwood, all the while making a great noise like thunder as it burst into fragments. Then, when silence had returned to Tamoanchan, the pieces of the Great Tree began to seep blood.

Ometeotl looked upon the ruins of the Great Tree, and they were greatly saddened. They saw that it was Xochiquetzal who had caused the death of the Tree, and so they sent Xochiquetzal out of Tamoanchan, never to return. Xochiquetzal left the home of the gods and went to live on earth. But no longer was she a goddess of joy and bright colors. Instead, she went about weeping and mourning, and her name was changed to Ixnextli, which means "Ashen Eyes," for she wept so long and so heavily that she became blinded by her tears.

The Fate of Souls

The Florentine Codex *is an important early modern record of Aztec history, religion, and culture. A twelve-volume ethnography written in Nahuatl by Fray Bernardino de Sahagún, a Franciscan missionary to Mexico, the codex was created between 1545 and de Sahagún's death in 1590 and was originally titled* Historia general de las cosas de Nueva España (General History of the Things of New Spain). *In the third volume of this ethnography, de Sahagún describes Aztec funerary customs and beliefs about the afterlife. The information he presents in his ethnography as reportage and descriptions has been reworked and presented here in story form, adopting the conceit of an elder addressing a child.*

And so, my child, you wish to know what happens to us when we die? Listen well, and I shall tell you, for the fate of our bodies and our souls is varied and is in the care of the gods themselves.

First, we shall speak of those who die of disease, for this is a fate that takes many of us from this earth. The souls of these people go first to Mictlan, to the Land of the Dead, where they are greeted by the Lord and Lady of Mictlan, Mictlantecuhtli and his consort Mictecacihuatl. To these dead the Lord of Mictlan will say, "Come into thy new abode, for here I have prepared a place for thee."

But do not think that it is easy to cross from the land of the living into Mictlan and to come before Mictlantecuhtli and his lady wife. Oh, no. It is not easy at all. Many dangers and pains must the soul endure before it is welcomed into its final home.

When the soul leaves its body, first it comes to a pass between two mountains. There is a road there that the soul must follow, and the road is watched by a great serpent. And when the road has been walked, the soul will come to a place that is watched by a great lizard. If the soul passes the serpent and lizard safely, it then must walk across eight deserts, and it is a long and lonely walk. After the soul traverses the deserts, it must climb over eight great hills, and this is a walk of great weariness and toil. Last of all, and most difficult of all, is a place where the winds are made of obsidian blades and stones, and by these the soul is slashed and buffeted. But if all is borne well, then the soul comes to Mictlan and is greeted by Mictlantecuhtli.

And it is to help the souls of our dead to pass through all these hardships in safety that we dress them in special paper clothing and burn with them the things they used in life, for these will be armor for them against the serpent, the lizard, and the obsidian wind. We put into their mouths a piece of obsidian to become a new heart for them in the land of the dead, and to our very great ones we give a piece of jade. Our brave warriors we burn with their swords and mantles and the spoils they have taken from our enemies. Our women we burn with their baskets and weaving tools, with their thread and their combs. Those who die with many goods are well protected, but alas for those who die in poverty! For they will not have the things they need to fend off the dangers on the path to Mictlan, and they will suffer much by the obsidian wind. But with all we send a small dog to act as their guide. We sacrifice the dog to the gods and burn it on the pyre with our loved ones. This is so when the soul reaches the nine rivers of Mictlan, the dog can guide it across in safety.

Once the soul passes through all the dangers and crosses the nine rivers, then it comes into the presence of the great Mictlantecuhtli. And O my child, what a thing it is to come before that god, with his blood-spattered skeleton body and necklace all made out of eyes! To him the dead offer their paper clothing, the incense, and other offerings that were burned on their pyres. To him the men give their breechcloths and the women their dresses. And thus, the soul of the dead one enters into Mictlan.

But think not that the journey of the soul is ended there! For it is not. Another great river there is to cross, and the living on earth must send more gifts to the Lord of Mictlan before their loved ones are allowed to move on. After eighty days, we burn more clothing, and again after two years, and three, and four. And when the dead have been four years waiting and when Mictlantecuhtli has received the gifts of the four years, only then does he permit the soul to go into the nine realms of the dead.

The soul goes to the bank of the last great river and there waits for a guide. For on the opposite bank there are a great many dogs, white and black and yellow, and only a dog can ferry the soul across. But the white dogs will not carry souls, for they say they have just bathed and do not wish to soil their coats. The black dogs will not carry souls, for they have made themselves unclean and must bathe first. The yellow dogs will leap into the water and ferry the souls across. And once the soul has been taken to the other side of that river, it is destroyed.

So much for the souls who die of disease.

What is that, my child? Why, yes, there are other deaths than by disease, and by and by I will tell you what happens to those souls.

Some people die when they are struck by thunderbolts. Others drown in water. Others die of leprosy or tumors or dropsy, while others die of diseases they get when men lie with women. Those who die of any of those causes go to a place called Tlalocan. O my child, Tlalocan is a pleasant place indeed. Maize and squash grow in abundance, and there one may eat one's fill of tomatoes and chilis and amaranth, for there it is always spring, and the tlaloque, the lords of thunder and rain, are there to receive the souls that come to Tlalocan.

The bodies of these dead we do not burn, but rather we bury them. But first we adorn them fittingly for their journey. We paint their faces with liquid rubber and amaranth paste. We put blue paper on their foreheads. We make a lock of hair of paper, and this we affix to the back of their heads. And thus adorned they enter Tlalocan. Also, we put into their graves images of mountains, like the ones in Tlalocan, and we dress them with capes and give them staves to help them on their journey there.

But the best home for the soul is reserved to our very bravest warriors who have died in battle and for those who are offered in

34

sacrifice to the gods. For these have died the noblest of all deaths and they are rewarded by being given a place in the house of the sun.

And the house of the sun is not a house such as we live in, but rather it is a wide plain where there is much maguey cactus and many mesquites, and the souls who dwell there watch the sun as it rises each day. Those who died with many piercings in their shields have the honor of being able to look the sun in its face, for they died most bravely. Those whose shields were not pierced have not this honor. A further honor is bestowed on those who died in battle or in sacrifice: when the living makes offerings to them, the offerings are conveyed to the souls for their use and enjoyment.

But even these souls do not stay long in the house of the sun. For after four years have passed, they are transformed into all manner of bright birds. They become hummingbirds, with their emerald and ruby plumage. They become the coztotol bird, with its yellow head, breast, and stomach. They become butterflies of every pattern and hue, and they come back to earth to drink of the sweet nectar in the flowers.

And now, my child, you know the fates of those who die upon this earth, and how we who are left behind must honor them and the gods.

PART II: AZTEC POLITICAL MYTHS

Huitzilopochtli and the Founding of Tenochtitlan

This is the origin tale of the Aztec people which tells how they migrated from a place far to the north under the guidance of the god of war, Huitzilopochtli. As with many myths, this one likely contains grains of historical truth. Linguists argue that Nahuatl, the language spoken by the Aztecs, likely originated in the southwestern United States, since as part of the Uto-Aztecan language family, it is related to Native American languages such as Hopi, Shoshoni, and Paiute.

Some scholars posit that the figure of Huitzilopochtli may originally have been a mortal human leader who later came to be deified, and certainly the origin story of Huitzilopochtli told here is different from that found in the "Legend of the Suns." But regardless of how this god was inserted into the Aztec pantheon, it would seem that it was during the reign of Itzcoatl (c. 1427 or 1428 to 1440 AD) that his worship became foregrounded in Aztec religion, along with the idea that blood sacrifice was supremely necessary to the proper honoring of the gods. This may have been at the instigation of Itzcoatl's general, a brilliant military man named Tlacaelel. Timothy Roberts, in his book on Mayan, Inca, and Aztec myth, states that the Aztec

36

migration myth, which relies heavily upon the power of Huitzilopochtli, was the creation of the Itzcoatl regime, as part of the emperor's program of rewriting history to favor Aztec power and ascendancy.

Long, long ago, far to the north, there was a place called Aztlan, which means "Place of the White Heron." In Aztlan there were seven tribes, and they all lived together in peace. Aztlan was a land of plenty. The soil grew fine crops of maize, and the waters teemed with fish and waterfowl. But best of all was the great mountain at the center of Aztlan. This mountain had the power to restore people their lost youth. At the base of the mountain was old age, while infancy was at the very summit. When the people felt they were becoming too old, they would climb the mountain to the age they wanted to attain and wait there until their bodies became youthful again. When they had the youth they desired, they would go back down the mountain and rejoin the people.

For many long years, the seven tribes lived together in Aztlan, enjoying the fruits of the earth and the long lives given by the sacred mountain. But word came to the ears of the people of Aztlan that to their south was a new place, one that had a great lake between the mountains, a place with rich soil for farming and plentiful obsidian for tools. One by one, the tribes left Aztlan in quest of this new place, until finally only one tribe was left, the Mexica, who later would take the name "Aztecs," meaning "People from Aztlan." The Mexica were saddened that they had been left in Aztlan all alone. They wanted to join the other tribes at the lake in the south to find a good, new life there, but there was no one among them who might lead them. And so, they remained in Aztlan, living as they had always done, but ever yearning to make the journey southwards.

Now, while six of the tribes of Aztlan were making their way to their new home in the south and while the Mexica languished in Aztlan waiting for a leader, the goddess Coatlicue (Serpent-Skirt), was busy about her home on Coatepec, the sacred Serpent Mountain. Dressed in the skirt of living serpents that gave her her name and a necklace made of severed human hearts, severed heads, and severed hands, the goddess went about her work. She took her broom in her clawed hands and went outside to sweep her patio. While she was sweeping, a beautiful ball of feathers came floating down through the air towards her. The feathers glinted and shone in brilliant greens, reds, and yellows. Coatlicue had never seen something so colorful, and she desired to keep it. The goddess put out her hand to catch the pretty thing, and when she had caught it, she tucked it away into her clothing.

Finally, Coatlicue finished all her work. She put her cleaning tools away and went to take the ball of feathers out so that she could look at it more closely. But no matter how she searched, she could not find it; the ball had disappeared. Not long afterward, Coatlicue found that she was with child. This was puzzling; she had not lain with a man in a very long time, certainly not recently enough that she would find herself in this state. She thought about how this might have come about and realized that somehow the feathered ball had entered her, making a new child grow in her womb.

As the months went on, Coatlicue's belly swelled. Soon all could see that she was with child. This greatly angered her four hundred sons, the Centzon Huitznahua (Four Hundred Southerners), and her daughters Coyolxauhqui (Precious Bells) and Malinalxochitl (Wild Grass Flower). They knew that their father, the hunter-god Mixcoatl (Cloud Serpent), had been away for a very long time, and so they thought that their mother had been unfaithful to him. They gathered outside Coatlicue's house, threatening to kill her if she did not tell them who she had lain with. But Coatlicue did not know who the father of her baby was, only that she had gotten the child from the ball of feathers, and so she did not answer her children.

"What shall I do?" said Coatlicue. "I am not a warrior. My children are many, and I am alone."

Coatlicue began to weep. Then from her womb she heard the voice of her unborn child. "Do not fear, Mother," he said. "It is I, your child, the god Huitzilopochtli, the Hummingbird of the South, and I will protect you from all dangers."

At this, Coatlicue felt greatly comforted. Meanwhile, the Centzon Huitznahua and their sisters paced outside their mother's house, shouting that they would surely kill her for dishonoring their family. But before they could enter the house, the baby leaped from Coatlicue's womb. Huitzilopochtli came forth fully grown and armed as a warrior. He descended upon his brothers and sisters, slashing with his weapon. The young god slew many of his brothers. Huitzilopochtli also slew his sister, Coyolxauhqui, cutting off her head and chopping her body into pieces and throwing them about the base of the sacred Serpent Mountain. Only a few of his brothers and his sister, Malinalxochitl, escaped, running away southwards.

Coatlicue was grateful that Huitzilopochtli had saved her from the wrath of her sons, but she grieved at the death of her daughter. Huitzilopochtli went to his mother and said, "Do not mourn, Mother. See? I will make it so that you can see your daughter's face every night." Then he took the head of his sister Coyolxauhqui and threw it with all his might into the heavens, and this is how the moon was made.

Word of Huitzilopochtli's great deeds came to the ears of the Mexica in Aztlan. They took counsel among themselves and decided that they would ask the god to be their leader and to take them to the lake in the south where the other tribes of Aztlan had already gone. Huitzilopochtli readily agreed to do this thing, and so when preparations were complete, the Mexica left their home in Aztlan and began the long journey to the good place by the lake.

After a time, the Mexica came to a place called Patzcuaro. Patzcuaro was a very pleasant place in the land of Michoacán. It had many lakes and much good land, and so the Mexica stopped there to rest a while. Some of the people, both men and women, went down to the edge of one of the lakes. On the shore of the lake, they undressed, and then went to bathe in the cool water, for the day was hot and their journey had been long. "Surely this is a very good place," they said to one another, "and we should make this our home."

But this was not the home to which Huitzilopochtli was leading the Mexica, although he agreed it was a good place and worthy of settlement. And so, he told the others who had stayed out of the water to go and steal the clothing of the ones who were bathing, so that they might not be able to follow when Huitzilopochtli led the rest on the next part of the journey.

Onwards the Mexica journeyed with Huitzilopochtli, looking for their new home at the good place by the lake. Now, among the people who were journeying southwards was Malinalxochitl, the sister of Huitzilopochtli, who had survived the day of his wrath against his half-siblings. Malinalxochitl was a beautiful sorceress who had the power to command all manner of venomous creatures such as snakes, scorpions, and spiders. She was jealous of the honor her brother had from the people and thought that she also should have the reverence due a divine being. She used her powers to threaten the people and to torment them. Soon the people begged Huitzilopochtli to rid them of her, for they were frightened and tired of her tricks and abuse. Huitzilopochtli told the people that they would make camp and then in the middle of the night they would depart while Malinalxochitl was sleeping, so that she would not know where they had gone. The people agreed this was a good plan, and so they did as Huitzilopochtli said.

Malinalxochitl slept soundly through the night, not realizing that everyone else had left. In the morning, she woke and found herself completely alone. She raged at her brother's betrayal and vowed revenge against him. But instead of trying to find where he and the Mexica had gone, she decided to stay in that place and found her own city, which she called Malinalco.

The Mexica continued walking southwards, until they came to the sacred Serpent Mountain, Coatepec, where Huitzilopochtli was born. A river flowed through the place, and so Huitzilopochtli instructed the Mexica to build a dam so that a lake might form in the low parts of the place. The Mexica did as the god commanded, and soon the place had a fine lake, full of fish and wildfowl, with rushes growing all around it. Thus, the place was named Tula, which means "Place of the Rushes."

Now, Huitzilopochtli had never intended the Mexica to stay there forever, for the good place by the lake was still a long way away. The god had told them to build the dam and make the lake so that they might see what awaited them when they finished their journey and so that they might have a good place to rest, for they had come a long way and had further yet to go. But the people saw how lovely Tula was, how plentiful the game was, and how beautiful the trees, and soon some of them began saying that they would rather stay there than continue on their journey, and they tried to convince the others that they should settle here and make it their home forever. This angered Huitzilopochtli, for it was not the place to which he was leading them, and it was not the place that was their destiny.

That night, the people's rest was disturbed by the sound of anguished cries. In the morning, they went to investigate, and in the place where the cries had come from, they found the bodies of those who had been urging the people to stay at Tula. Each one of the bodies had been ripped open and their hearts torn out by Huitzilopochtli.

The god then called the people to him and ordered them to take down the dam they had built. The pent-up waters rushed forth at first, but soon the river returned to its bed. No longer was Tula a place of shade and plenty. The rushes and reeds dried up. The fish died flopping and gasping on the desert sand. The waterfowl flew away. And so, the Mexica had to leave and continue their journey to the good place by the lake that Huitzilopochtli had promised to them.

Long and long the Mexica journeyed. There had been marriages among them and babies born. And the babies had grown into children and the children into men and women who made marriages and had their own children in turn. And so, there came a time when

41

there were very few who remembered their old home in Aztlan and those were most aged, and still the Mexica had not reached the end of their journey to the good place by the lake.

Eventually they came to a place called Chapultepec, which means "Hill of the Locusts." Chapultepec was on the shores of Lake Texcoco. The Mexica made camp there, but they were afraid for the people of that region were hostile and unwelcoming. The people of Chapultepec were led by Copil, the son of Malinalxochitl, who had been raised to manhood on the story of Huitzilopochtli's betrayal and abandonment of his mother and who therefore had a hatred of the Mexica and their god. But Huitzilopochtli told his people to be of stout heart, for he did not mean for them to stay there long. The god also told them that if they were to be the truly great people he wanted them to become, they would have to face enemies and defeat them, for in this way they would show their own strength and courage not only to others but to themselves.

Copil, meanwhile, went to all the peoples in the nearby land. He told them that the Mexica were not honorable, that they were not trustworthy, that their customs were disgusting and reprehensible, and that they were warlike and meant to attack at any moment. Soon he had aroused all of the people in the district to hate the Mexica. The people of Chapultepec and their allies raised an army. They attacked the Mexica, and a fierce battle ensued. Copil's army was victorious, but Copil himself was captured. Huitzilopochtli cut open Copil's chest and tore out his beating heart, then threw it far out into the lake, where it came to rest on a small island.

Although Copil's army left the Mexica alone after the death of their leader, the Mexica saw that they could not stay in Chapultepec. Huitzilopochtli led them next to a place farther south on the other side of the lake. This place was called Culhuacan, a prosperous city ruled by a mighty king. When the Mexica arrived, they asked Huitzilopochtli what they ought to do, for they had not forgotten the battle at Chapultepec and they did not want to make enemies in this new place. Huitzilopochtli answered them, saying, "Make an embassy to the king of this place. Ask him for some land where our people might settle and thrive. Whatever he gives to you, take it, whether it is good or bad."

The Mexica therefore chose an embassy from among their elders and brave men and sent them to meet with the king of Culhuacan. The king himself received them graciously and listened to their plea for land where they might settle. But his advisers did not look kindly on the Mexica, and they told the king to send them away. When the king refused to do this inhospitable thing, his advisers told him to give the Mexica land in a place called Tizapan. The king agreed to this and told the Mexica embassy where the place was and how they might get there. The ambassadors thanked him for his kindness and went back to their own people, where they told Huitzilopochtli what had passed between them and the king of Culhuacan. Huitzilopochtli then told the people to gather up their belongings and make ready to go to Tizapan.

When the Mexica arrived there, they were much saddened for the land the king gave them was poor. What is more, it was on the edge of a swamp and infested with great swarms of insects and a multitude of venomous serpents. But Huitzilopochtli told his people to be of good courage for he would show them a way to make Tizapan a goodly place to live. First, he showed them how to capture the insects and cook them for food, and soon there were so few insects that the Mexica were hardly troubled by them at all. Then the god showed the people how to do the same with the serpents, and in a short time all of them had been eaten as well. Once all the vermin had been consumed, the Mexica set about building a settlement, with farms and homes and a temple.

After a time, it came to the ears of the king that the Mexica had made a settlement in Tizapan and appeared to be prospering. The king would not credit these stories for he knew that Tizapan was a most inhospitable place. But he wanted to see whether the stories were indeed true, so he sent messengers to Tizapan to give the Mexica his greetings and ask how they did. The messengers came back to the king saying that they had seen fertile fields and a well-ordered town, and that the Mexica thanked the king for his generosity in giving them the land for their settlement. They also asked whether they might be allowed to enter Culhuacan to trade with the people there and to make marriages with the inhabitants.

The king listened well to all the messengers told him. He took careful thought about the requests the Mexica had made. Then he agreed to allow them to trade and to marry, for he saw that they were indeed a hardy people and he deemed it most unwise to make enemies of them. Indeed, the king went so far as to ask the aid of the Mexica in his fight against a nearby people called the Xochimilco. The Mexica sent their warriors willingly, and so they helped the king of Culhuacan to victory. And so it was that the Mexica and the people of Culhuacan lived peaceably together for a time.

Huitzilopochtli saw that the Mexica had made a good home for themselves in Tizapan. He saw that they had begun to think of their settlement as a permanent home. But Tizapan was not the good place by the lake that he had promised them. And the Mexica needed to face yet more hardship before they could become the rulers of the land as Huitzilopochtli intended. They needed to find some reason to fight with the people of Culhuacan, to get themselves expelled from that land, before they truly thought of it as their home and could not be persuaded to leave. So, the god called to himself his priests and told them that they were to go to the king of Culhuacan and ask him for one of his daughters, that he might marry her. The priests did what Huitzilopochtli asked of them, and when the king heard that his daughter was to be the bride of a god, he readily agreed and sent his daughter to Tizapan.

When the young woman arrived, Huitzilopochtli told his priests to bring her to the temple and make her a sacrifice. Then they were to flay the girl and place her skin on one of the priests, who was to pretend to be the young woman as if she were still alive. After all that had been done, Huitzilopochtli sent messengers to Culhuacan to invite the king and his court to attend the wedding ceremony between himself and the king's daughter. The king rejoiced at this invitation. He collected many fine gifts to give the god and his wife. But when he arrived at Culhuacan, he was horrified to see one of the priests of Huitzilopochtli doing ritual dances dressed in the skin of his daughter.

The king of Culhuacan and his nobles ran back to their city, where the king summoned to him all his army. Then he led them on an attack against the Mexica. The Mexica fought so well and so bravely that the king and his army were forced to retreat. But the Mexica knew that they could no longer stay in Tizapan, so they went further along the lakeshore to a place called Ixtapalapan, where they made camp. Even though they had been victorious against the army from Culhuacan, the Mexica were in great distress, for yet again had they been driven out of a place that they had settled and begun to think of as home.

Huitzilopochtli saw the distress of his people, so he said to them, "Be of good cheer. Your long journey is nearly ended. You will know where your final home is when you see this sign: on an island in the lake, the one where I threw the heart of your enemy, Copil, you will see a nopal cactus. Atop the cactus there will be a great eagle, holding a white serpent in its talons. That island is to be your home. On that island, you will build a great city, and you will call it Tenochtitlan, the Place of the Nopal Cactus."

Then Huitzilopochtli told the Mexica to take their rest and that in the morning they would go in search of the island with its cactus. When the sun rose, the people ate a hurried meal and then began searching along the lakeshore for the island the god had told them of. After many hours, one of the priests cried out and pointed towards the middle of the lake. There on an island not far from shore was a nopal cactus, and atop the cactus was a great eagle, holding a white serpent in its talons, just as Huitzilopochtli had said. The people rejoiced greatly and fell down in homage to the great bird. The eagle saw the people doing it honor, and it bowed to them in turn. This increased the joy of the Mexica, for it told them that they had finally come to the end of their journey and that their future was surely to be a prosperous and blessed one.

And this is the tale of how the god Huitzilopochtli was born and how he led the Mexica to their new home in Tenochtitlan, which became the center of the mighty Aztec Empire.

Motecuhzoma I and the Search for Chicomoztoc

One place where history and myth collide is in this tale of the search for Chicomoztoc, which means "Place of the Seven Caves." Chicomoztoc is one of the mythical places of origin for the Aztec people, and according to this legend the search was undertaken at the command of Motecuhzoma I (r. 1440-1469 AD), the successor to Itzcoatl. This search may never have actually happened, and even if it did, it is certain that Motecuhzoma's emissaries did not find the mystical mountain of youth or the goddess Coatlicue, mother of Huitzilopochtli. It seems likely that this myth, like that of the Aztec migration and those about the fall of the Toltecs, was constructed as part of the effort to elevate Aztec culture and legitimize Aztec rule in the years following the creation of the Triple Alliance under Itzcoatl.

In this story, we also see the central place of cacao beans (Nahuatl cacahuatl, *but the word originally was Mayan) and chocolate (Nahuatl* chocolatl) *as a luxury item in Aztec culture. So valuable were cacao beans that they even were used as a form of currency and demanded as tribute. Although today we tend to eat or drink chocolate as a sweetened food, early Mesoamerican cultures including the Aztecs and Mayans usually drank chocolate bitter, often flavored with chilis, vanilla, or spices, and sometimes thickened with maize.*

One day, the Emperor Motecuhzoma (Angry Like a Lord) bethought himself of the ancestors of the Aztecs and of the great tale of their journey from Aztlan to Lake Texcoco and all the deeds they had done. He bethought himself also of the great god Huitzilopochtli who, like the Aztecs, had left his own home and his own mother behind in order to guide the Aztecs and help them achieve greatness in their new home of Tenochtitlan. Motecuhzoma remembered that Huitzilopochtli had promised his mother, the goddess Coatlicue, that he would return, but he had not done so; rather, he had stayed in Tenochtitlan to look after the Aztecs and to receive the worship he was due as a mighty god and protector of his people. Motecuhzoma wondered whether Coatlicue was still alive and whether she had received any news of her son.

The emperor therefore sought the advice of his chief general, a man named Tlacaelel, who besides being the bravest warrior and best strategist the Aztecs had ever known was also a pious man and learned in the history of his people. Motecuhzoma called Tlacaelel before him and said, "I have in mind a great deed to be done by our bravest men. I want them to go in search of Chicomoztoc, the Place of the Seven Caves, where our people first lived many ages ago. I want to send many warriors, well equipped, to find Aztlan and its sacred mountain and to see whether Coatlicue the Serpent-Skirted is still alive and to bring her tidings of our people and of her mighty son, Huitzilopochtli. I wish that these men bring with them many fine gifts to be given to Coatlicue, to show her our gratitude and the strength and prosperity of the Aztec people and that she may know the true might and worth of her son."

"O Mighty One," said Tlacaelel, "surely this is a great and blessed deed that you propose and will bring much honor to you, to our people, and to the god Huitzilopochtli. But if you ask for my advice on how this might be accomplished, I say this: do not send warriors, for they will not be able to find Aztlan, nor will they be able to find Coatlicue the Serpent-Skirted. Our warriors are worthy and courageous, but all their skills will not avail them in this venture. No, if you would follow my advice, I would tell you to send sorcerers and wise men, for only they know the way to find such a place as Aztlan.

"For as our scholars tell us, this place was most delightful and a land of plenty when our people dwelled there, even though it was in a marsy land; but then it became wild and overgrown with reeds, brambles, and trees with long thorns, and the ground was stony and infertile when our people departed it to seek a new home elsewhere. Aztlan will not be easily found, even by our doughtiest men, and even should they find it, the trees themselves will turn against them and keep them away.

"Also, by sending soldiers armed for battle we may frighten the people of Aztlan, which is not desirable. Neither would we want to make Coatlicue fear your emissaries. Rather we should send men who are wise and learned, those who will know how to speak to the people of Aztlan and to Coatlicue in a manner befitting an embassy from one great nation to another. These also should be sorcerers with much knowledge of how such a place as Aztlan might be reached by magic."

Motecuhzoma listened carefully to all Tlacaelel said, and he agreed that this was sage advice. The emperor therefore called to him Cuauhcoatl (Eagle Serpent), who was the royal historian and a very aged and learned man. Motecuhzoma asked Cuauhcoatl to tell him the story of Chicomoztoc and all he knew about Aztlan and the place where Huitzilopochtli dwelt before he led the Aztecs on their great journey.

"O Mighty One," said Cuauhcoatl, "I will do my best to tell you all I know, that your royal purpose might be accomplished with great success. The place our ancestors dwelt was called 'Aztlan,' which means 'Place of the White Heron.' As our scholars tell us, in Aztlan there is a great lake, and in the midst of this lake is a great hill called Colhuacan, which means 'Twisted Hill,' because its summit is twisted all round. This hill is where the Seven Caves are located, and it was from these caves that our ancestors first emerged into the world, and it was in these caves where they first lived. Our ancestors called themselves 'Mexica' and 'Aztecs,' which are names we still use proudly today.

"We know that Aztlan was a place of plenty and ease. The people ate freely of the many kinds of waterfowl that dwelt there along with a great multitude of fish. Beautiful trees grew all about the place, giving shade to all who sought it. The gardens of our ancestors were fertile and easily worked, yielding maize, amaranth, tomatoes, beans, and all kinds of chilis; we know these still today, for those who departed Aztlan on the great journey brought seeds with them, and we, their descendants, still farm those good plants in our own gardens.

"As we do today, our ancestors went about in canoes upon the water. They delighted in the songs and colored feathers of many birds. They drew cool, refreshing water from many springs. Their life in Aztlan was altogether delightful.

"But once our ancestors left Aztlan, they found that the land was not so easily worked and that food was not so easily found. The ground was stony, dry, and overgrown with brambles. There were many venomous serpents and dangerous animals that did the people harm. It was a long and hard road that brought our people from Aztlan to the prosperous place we live in today."

When Cuauhcoatl finished his tale, Motecuhzoma thanked him for his wisdom and then said, "I think what you have told me must be true, for it is the same tale that Tlacaelel has told me. I now command that messengers be sent through our lands that they might find sixty sorcerers who have the skill and knowledge to accomplish the task I will set them. The sorcerers are to be brought here, that I may give them their instructions."

And so, it was done as Motecuhzoma commanded. Not long thereafter, the sixty sorcerers were found and assembled before the emperor to hear his will. Motecuhzoma said to the sorcerers, "I welcome you here, honored elders, for I have a mighty task for you. I wish that you go forth to find Aztlan, the land from which our ancestors came, to see whether it still exists. I also wish that you find Coatlicue the Serpent-Skirted to see whether she yet lives and to bring her news of her mighty son, Huitzilopochtli. I have heard from my wise advisers that finding this place will be difficult and that your skills are what is needed to carry out my commands. Therefore, prepare yourselves in whatever way necessary, so that you may meet with success on your road."

Motecuhzoma then commanded that many rich gifts be prepared for the sorcerers to take with them: mantles made of many colored feathers or woven from the finest cotton, beautiful women's clothing sewn with the greatest of care, gold, jewels; cacao, cotton, vanilla, and the brightest and most colorful feathers in the whole kingdom. These were to be given to Coatlicue and the people of Aztlan as tokens of goodwill from the Aztecs. To the sorcerers themselves Motecuhzoma gave colorful mantles and many other good things, along with enough food to nourish them during their journey.

Taking all these things from the emperor, the sorcerers promised to do their utmost to carry out his commands. They then departed the fair city of Tenochtitlan and went to the hill called Coatepec that stands near the city of Tula. When they arrived at Coatepec, they climbed the hill, and there on its summit they began to work their magic, for they knew it was by magic alone that they might find Chicomoztoc and Aztlan. They covered their bodies with magical ointments. They drew magical symbols upon the ground. They called to the many spirits they knew who could give them the power to go to Aztlan. The spirits replied by turning the sorcerers into birds and beasts, such as jaguars and ocelots, and then whisked them away to the place of Aztlan.

The sorcerers arrived at the shores of the lake Cuauhcoatl had described, and there they were turned back into their human forms by the spirits. Looking out over the lake, the sorcerers saw the hill of Colhuacan. They also saw many people in canoes. Some were fishing. Others tended their chinampas, the floating garden plots that the Aztecs of Tenochtitlan also used to grow their food. All seemed happy and prosperous. Then one of the people looked up from her work and cried out, "Look! There are strangers on the shore."

The people paddled their canoes to the place where the sorcerers stood. They heard the sorcerers speaking quietly amongst themselves of all the wonders they were seeing and of what they should say, and the people were astonished that the strangers spoke their own language.

When the people were close enough to the sorcerers to speak without shouting, one of them said, "Who are you? Where do you come from, and what is your business here?"

The sorcerers said, "We are Aztecs. We are ambassadors of our emperor, and we are looking for the place our people came from."

The people asked, "Which god is yours?"

"We honor the great Huitzilopochtli," said the sorcerers, "and we are ambassadors sent by the Emperor Motecuhzoma, bearing gifts for Coatlicue the Serpent-Skirted and to bring her news of her son if she yet lives, and to find Chicomoztoc, the ancient home of our people."

Upon hearing this, one of the people was dispatched to find the one who cared for Coatlicue, mother of Huitzilopochtli. They explained the errand of the sorcerers to the guardian, who was a very aged man. "Let them come here," said the guardian, "and make them most welcome, for they are our kin."

And so, the people took the sorcerers into their canoes and paddled them across the lake to the hill of Colhuacan. At the foot of the hill was the house of the guardian. The sorcerers went to him and said, "Honorable Father, we are ambassadors from our emperor, and we humbly ask your permission to speak to her who is the mother of our god."

"You are very welcome here," said the guardian. "Tell me, who was it that sent you here? What is the name of your emperor?"

The sorcerers told the guardian that Motecuhzoma was their emperor, and that he and his trusted adviser, Tlacaelel, had commanded them to undertake the journey to Aztlan.

When the guardian heard this, his brow furrowed. "Motecuhzoma and Tlacaelel? I know not those names. Tell me, are there still among you Tezacatetl or Acacitli? Ocelopan or Ahuatl? Xomimitl, Ahuexotl, or Huicton? Is Tenoch still alive? For these were the leaders of those who departed this land long ago, and we have heard nothing of them since then. Nor have we heard anything of the four who bore the god Huitzilopochtli away from here."

"Venerable One," said the sorcerers, "We have heard those names, but we do not know any of those men for they died long ago."

"Oh!" said the guardian. "Oh, what sad news you bring! How did they die? How is it that they are dead while we yet live? Who leads you now that they are gone? And who is it that cares for Huitzilopochtli?"

"The grandsons of your friends are our leaders," said the sorcerers, "and the priest of Huitzilopochtli is a very wise and holy man named Cuauhcoatl, who serves the god well and lets us know his will."

"Ah, that is good that the god is well looked after by a devout man," said the guardian. "Did you see him yourselves before you came here? Did he send a message?"

The sorcerers told the guardian that Motecuhzoma and Tlacaelel were the ones who had sent them on their mission. Then they had to admit that they had not spoken to Huitzilopochtli themselves, nor had the god given them any messages.

"That is vexing," said the guardian, "for when Huitzilopochtli left us, he said that he would be returning, and we have had no word as to when that will be. His mother has been waiting all this time, and she weeps daily because she has had no news. You should go and speak to her, for maybe you can bring her comfort."

"Indeed, we would be honored to speak with the Serpent-Skirted One," said the sorcerers, "for that is part of our mission, and we have many fine gifts to offer her."

The old man then told the sorcerers to take up their bundles of gifts and to follow him to the house of Coatlicue, which was near the top of the hill. Now, the upper part of the hill was made of very soft sand, and the old guardian walked up with great ease. But the sorcerers foundered under the weight of their burdens, their feet sinking down into the sand. The guardian noticed that the sorcerers were lagging behind him. He looked back and saw them struggling through the sand. "Why is this difficult?" he said. "Try to go faster."

The sorcerers tried and tried to do as the guardian said, but the only result was that they sank up to their waists in the sand and could not go any farther. The guardian went back to where the sorcerers were and said, "What have you been eating that you are too heavy to walk this hill?"

"We eat the food that grows in our gardens," replied the sorcerers, "and we drink chocolate."

"Ah, that is what is wrong," said the guardian. "Your food is too rich and too heavy. You should live more simply, as we do here. Then you would be able to walk this hill. But since you cannot, you must give me your bundles and wait here while I go see whether Coatlicue will come down to speak with you."

And so, the old man picked up a bundle of gifts the sorcerers had brought, and carrying it on his back as though it weighed less than a handful of feathers, he walked up the hill to the house of Coatlicue. There he set down the bundle, and then he went back to fetch the rest. The old man carried each of bundle up the hill on his back with the greatest of ease.

When all the gifts had been brought to the house, Coatlicue herself came down the hill to meet with the sorcerers. She was old, old, old and not one speck of beauty was in her face or her body. Her hair was matted, her skin and clothing were covered with filth, and she wept many sorrowful tears.

"I bid you welcome, O my sons," said the goddess, "and I beg your pardon for my appearance. But it is grief for my son that makes me like this, for I have neither bathed nor combed my hair nor changed my clothing since he departed, and I have spent my days in weeping, awaiting his return. Tell me, is it true that you have been sent here by the seven elders who went with the people that my beloved Huitzilopochtli led away from here all those long years ago?"

The ambassadors looked upon Coatlicue and her hideous aspect, and they were greatly afraid. They all bowed before her as best they could despite the sand and said, "O Great Lady, of the seven elders we know but the names, for they died long ago. The ones who sent us were Motecuhzoma, our king and your humble servant, and his trusted adviser, Tlacaelel, a man both wise and brave. They wished us to come here to give you their greetings and to see the place that our ancestors once called home.

"It has been many, many long years since our ancestors departed this place. Motecuhzoma is himself the fifth king of our people. The four who came before him were Acamapichtli, the first king, then Huitzilihuitl, then Chimalpopoca, and then Itzcoatl. Motecuhzoma bids us to say to you, 'I greet thee, O mother of our god, and I bow before thee as thy humble servant. My name is Huehue Motecuhzoma (Motecuhzoma the Elder), and anything thou biddest of me, so shall I do.'

"And our king also bids of us to tell you of the fate of our peoples, and what befell them after they left this place. They traveled long and far through many hardships. The people were often hungry and very poor, and for a long time they were vassals of others and forced to pay heavy tribute. But now we are masters of our own city, a beautiful and prosperous place. We have built many roads on which all may travel in safety. What is more, the Aztecs are the rulers of the land, our city is the principal capital, and others now pay us tribute. To show how prosperous our people have become, Motecuhzoma bids us give you these gifts, for they were won with great toil and with the aid of your mighty son, Huitzilopochtli, who now dwells among us in very great honor. And this is all the message we have been commanded to give to you."

When Coatlicue heard the message of the sorcerers, she ceased her weeping. "My sons, I bid you most welcome and give you all my thanks for these gifts and for the message you have given me. But I am greatly saddened to hear that the seven elders have passed from this world, and I wish to understand how that befell them for all their friends here are yet living.

"Also, I wish to know more of some of these gifts." She held up a bundle of cacao and asked, "What is this thing? Is it something to eat?"

"O Great Lady," replied the sorcerers, "that is cacao, and from it we make a delicious drink. We also mix it with other foods, and it is very good to eat that way."

"Ah, I see," said Coatlicue. "This is what has prevented you climbing the hill, for it is very heavy food." Then the goddess looked upon the mantles that Motecuhzoma had given the sorcerers and she said, "That is very fine raiment you wear. Does my son Huitzilopochtli wear anything like it? Does he also have clothing well woven and adorned with bright feathers?"

"Yes, indeed," said the sorcerers. "He is dressed this way and with even richer things than these mantles for he is much honored, and it is with his aid that we have won the wealth we now bring to you."

Coatlicue then said, "My children, my heart is much gladdened by your words and by the tale you tell of my son and of those who left this place long ago. It pleases me that the people now live in prosperity. But in return, I ask you to bear a message to Huitzilopochtli. Tell him to take pity on his mother, for I am lonely here now that he is gone. Tell him that he should remember his words to me when he left, that he said he would come back after he had led the seven tribes to a place of safety and prosperity, that he would go out and conquer many peoples and then come home to me when his own people were conquered in their turn.

"But it seems to me that my son has made a good home among you and that he is so content there and so well cared for that he forgets

55

his obligation to his mother." The goddess then gave to the sorcerers a simple mantle and breechcloth woven from maguey fibers, saying, "I bid you to take this mantle and this breechcloth and to give it to Huitzilopochtli as a gift from me and as a reminder that he promised to come back."

The sorcerers bowed to the goddess. They took the clothing with the promise that they would give it and her message to Huitzilopochtli as soon as they returned home. But before they went far, the goddess called to them. "Wait!" she said. "I will show you how it is that the people live so long and never grow old here. Look at my guardian. He is very old. But when he comes down to you, he will change into a young man."

And so, the old guardian began to walk down the mountain. As he walked, he gradually became younger and younger. When he reached the sorcerers, he said, "Now I appear to be about twenty years old. But when I go back up, I will become older."

The man started walking up the hill. When he was about halfway up, he seemed to be forty years old. Further up the hill, he became very old. Then he turned to the sorcerers and said, "See, O children, what this hill does for us. If an old person wants to be younger, he climbs to the point of the hill that will give him the age he wants to be. If he wants to be a boy again, he can climb to the very top. To be a young man, he need only climb a bit more than halfway. Climbing halfway makes one middle-aged. This is how we live a very long time, and I now understand that this is why the seven leaders who left with the people are no longer living; you have no such hill in your land, and they could not restore their youth.

"I think also it must be the way that you live in your land. You drink much cacao, you eat rich foods, and you wear fine clothing. All of this has made you heavy and slow, and it causes you to age. You show this in your bodies and in the gifts that you bore hither. However, you should not go back home without gifts. We will give you many of the things that we value to take back to your king."

56

The guardian then ordered gifts to be prepared for the sorcerers. The people of Aztlan gave them all kinds of waterfowl that lived around the lake that surrounded the hill, ducks and geese and herons. They gave many types of plants and flowers. The people of Aztlan prepared garlands of colorful flowers, good mantles, and breechcloths of maguey fiber, clothing of the type they wore, to be given to Motecuhzoma and Tlacaelel.

"Go now with good fortune," said the guardian, "and beg the pardon of your king and his noble adviser for the humble nature of the gifts you bear. They are nothing so fine as what you brought, but they are the very best that we have."

The sorcerers thanked the guardian and the people for their gifts and their hospitality. Then they began to make the magic that would take them back to their home. They painted their bodies with the magic ointments. They drew the mystical symbols on the ground. They summoned the spirits to take them back home.

The spirits came and turned them back into the animal forms in which the sorcerers came to Aztlan and whisked them away to the hill of Coatepec. When the sorcerers regained their human forms, they looked about them and were dismayed for some twenty of their number were missing. What became of those twenty was never discovered, but some say that they must have fallen prey to wild beasts on the journey back to Coatepec.

The sorcerers shouldered their bundles of gifts and set out for Tenochtitlan. When they arrived, they were given an audience with Motecuhzoma. They told the emperor what had happened in Aztlan and gave to him the many gifts that the guardian of Coatlicue and the people of Aztlan had given them. The sorcerers reported everything that had been said between them and the goddess and between them and her guardian. They told the emperor about the magical hill that could restore lost youth and that the people who lived in Aztlan today were the same ones who had stayed behind when the seven tribes left their homes on their great journey south so very long ago.

Also, they told the emperor what the goddess had said of her son, that she felt very lonely without him and wanted him to come home to her, and that she had said that one day he would do so because the kingdom of Tenochtitlan would be conquered, just as the Mexica had conquered the people who had lived there before they came.

Motecuhzoma thanked the sorcerers for their messages and their gifts. Then he summoned Tlacaelel to hear the sorcerers' report. They told him about all they had seen, the plants and the trees, the waterfowl and the fish, and the floating gardens that yielded every good thing in great plenty. They told Tlacaelel how the people navigated the lake in their canoes. They told him also that there seemed never to be only one growing season but many overlapping, so that while some maize was still sprouting, other fields were ready for harvest, and in this way, food was always very plentiful.

When all of that had been related, the sorcerers described their adventure on the hill of youth and how they could not climb it because they sank into the soft sand, but that the guardian could climb it with ease even though he was heavily burdened with the gifts they had brought for the goddess. They explained that they sank into the sand because they had been made heavy by their rich living and by drinking so much chocolate. The sorcerers also told the emperor and Tlacaelel how Coatlicue and the guardian had wept to hear that their friends who had left on the great journey south were now dead.

Motecuhzoma and Tlacaelel listened in wonder to the tale of the sorcerers. They were greatly moved to hear of all the beautiful things of the land of Aztlan and how their ancestors dwelt there still with the mother of their own god, and they sorrowed a little that they had not been able to see these things with their own eyes. Then the emperor and his adviser gravely thanked the sorcerers for the gifts and for having undertaken such a perilous journey. They ordered the sorcerers to be rewarded with many fine gifts. And when that had been done, they told the sorcerers to go to the temple of Huitzilopochtli and to clothe him in the mantle and breechcloth they bore with them, for these were the gifts his own mother had made and had sent just for him.

Huemac and the Sorcerer

Among the contents of the Florentine Codex, *Fray Bernardino de Sahagún's sixteenth-century ethnography of the Aztecs, are stories about Huemac, the mythical last king of the Toltecs and of Quetzalcoatl's exile from Tula. These are tales de Sahagún learned from his Aztec informants.*

One series of stories in the Florentine Codex *tells of the misfortunes of Huemac and of his people at the hands of the Aztec god, Tezcatlipoca. Although the primary characters in these stories are Toltecs, the stories themselves are Aztec creations intended to legitimize Aztec supremacy by providing mythical explanations for the fall of Toltec culture. In these legends, Tezcatlipoca comes in disguise to Tula, the capital city of the Toltecs, where he insinuates himself into Toltec society and then wreaks havoc, first by ensorcelling the people into destroying themselves and then finally by slaying them himself.*

Once there was a king of the Toltecs named Huemac. He had a daughter who was the most beautiful woman in all the land. Many men desired to marry her, but her father always forbade the match.

The great enemy of Huemac and of the Toltecs was the god of the Smoking Mirror, Tezcatlipoca. Tezcatlipoca was always looking for ways to cause trouble for the Toltecs, so he went to Tula disguised as the sorcerer Titlacauan. He changed himself into the form of a young man selling green chilis. He went about in this form without a breechcloth, so that his manhood was visible for all to see. Naked as he was, he went into the marketplace near the palace to sell his chilis.

While Titlacauan was selling chilis in the market, the daughter of Huemac happened to see him there. She saw him in his nakedness, along with the virility of his manhood, and was inflamed with a passion to have Titlacauan as her lover. So much in desire was she that she began to act as though she were ill, refusing food, sighing and groaning, and looking sad and unwell.

Huemac saw that his daughter was unwell, so he went to her maidservants to ask what was the matter. The maidservants told the king, "Your daughter saw that seller of green chilis in the marketplace. He goes about without a breechcloth, and she is now burning with desire for him."

Huemac therefore ordered that the seller of green chilis be brought before him to account for his behavior. Messengers went all through the city of Tula announcing that the man was wanted by the king. They looked high and low for him, but nowhere was the man to be found, until one day he reappeared in the marketplace in the very same spot where the king's daughter had first seen him. Word was sent to the king that the seller of chilis had returned, and the king commanded that the man be brought before him immediately. Not long afterward, the messengers returned with the man.

"Who are you, and where are you from?" asked Huemac.

"Oh, I'm just a stranger here. I sell green chilis in the marketplace," said Titlacauan.

Then Huemac said, "Where have you been before coming here? Also, it is indecent to go about with one's loins ungirt. Take a breechcloth and cover yourself."

Titlacauan replied "But in my land this is how we go about. We wear no breechcloths."

"I care not what you do in your own land," said Huemac. "You are now in my kingdom, and your nakedness has inflamed my daughter with desire. You must heal her of this ill."

Then the stranger became frightened. "Oh, no, great king. Do not force me to do this thing. I am merely a seller of green chilis."

"I care not," said the king. "You have made my daughter ill, so you shall heal her of it."

The king ordered that the man be taken away to be bathed and made comely for his daughter. And when this had been done, the king brought the man to his daughter and said, "There she is. Heal her."

And so Titlacauan lay with the king's daughter, and she was greatly satisfied thereby. When Huemac saw how happy his daughter was, he married her to Titlacauan. When word spread that the king had married his daughter to the seller of green chilis, the people began to make fun of the king because he had given his daughter to a stranger and not to one of his own people. Huemac was greatly shamed by this, so he came up with a plan to rid himself of the stranger once and for all. Huemac called to him his chief warriors. He ordered them to take the army and make war with Cacatepec and Coatepec, and while the fighting was well in hand, they would abandon Titlacauan on the field so that he would be either slain or taken prisoner. He also told the chief warriors to give Titlacauan only hunchbacks and others with unsound bodies to be his fellows in the battle.

And so, the Toltecs declared war on Coatepec and Cacatepec and set out to fight. The chief warriors set Titlacauan and the hunchbacks and others in one part of the field. Then the rest of them went to another part, thinking that the Coatepeca and Cacatepeca warriors would kill Titlacauan and his fellows. The hunchbacks and the others who were with Titlacauan were sorely afraid, for they knew they were not strong enough to fight the other warriors. But Titlacauan told them not to worry, for their enemies were sure to be defeated.

Once battle was joined, the Toltec warriors abandoned Titlacauan and went back to Tula. They told Huemac, "We left the stranger and his fellows alone on the field as you commanded. Surely they have all been killed by now."

But on the battlefield, Titlacauan cried out, "Fight fiercely! Be courageous! We will defeat them! I promise you that we will bring back many captives and slay that number over again!"

And when the Coatepeca and Cacatepeca warriors attacked Titlacauan and his fellows, they were taken captive and slain in great numbers. When the battle was done, Titlacauan and the others went back to Tula. Word had already come to Huemac of the deeds they had done, and word had also spread throughout the city. Titlacauan and his companions were met at the gates of Tula by a cheering crowd. They gave to Titlacauan bright quetzal feathers and the turquoise shield and many other trappings that are given to heroes and kings. The people danced and sang in Titlacauan's honor. They sounded their conch shell trumpets and beat their drums. And when the procession reached the gates of the palace, the people painted the faces of Titlacauan and his companions red, their bodies yellow, and placed feathers on their heads.

Huemac came forth to meet Titlacauan and his companions. "See, now the Toltecs greet you as a hero of the people and as one of them. Truly are you my son-in-law."

But Titlacauan had no thought for becoming one of the Toltecs. Even though he had defeated the Coatepeca and Cacatepeca, and even though he had been anointed with red and yellow paint and with feathers, he still planned to destroy the Toltecs. Now he turned to the crowds of people and thought to make them dance and sing. Titlacauan went to the summit of Tzatzitepetl, the Mountain That Speaks, that stood just outside the city. And from the top of that mountain, he called for everyone everywhere to come to Tula.

When everyone had assembled, Titlacauan went to a place called Texcalpan, and he told all the people to follow him. Then Titlacauan began to sing and beat his drum. Everyone began to dance together and to sing the song of Titlacauan. From sunset to midnight, Titlacauan led the singing and dancing, and no one sat apart from it.

The people were so intent on their songs and dances that they did not watch where they were going. Some of them fell into a canyon. They died when they hit the ground, and their bodies were turned into stones. Others had started crossing the bridge that went over the canyon, but Titlacauan broke the bridge, and everyone on it fell into the river below, where their bodies were turned into stones. But even as the people were falling into the canyon and into the river, still they did not understand that Titlacauan was making them sing and dance so they would destroy themselves.

There was another time when Titlacauan came to Tula and worked sorcery upon the people there. He disguised himself and came to Tula as a magician holding a small figurine in his hand. The figurine looked like a small child, but some say that this was the god Huitzilopochtli who had transformed himself. Titlacauan held the figurine up to the people, and lo! The figurine began to dance of its own accord.

The people were entranced by the dancing of this figurine. They crowded towards the magician, wanting to see more. So many people pushed forward towards the magician that some were crushed to death in the press of bodies, while others fell and were trampled underfoot and so died there. But the magician took no note of the crowds or of the cries and moans of the dying. Rather, he said to the people, "Look upon this sorcery! Surely it is by evil magic that this figurine is made to dance."

Then the people turned upon the magician. Instead of wanting to see the figurine dance, they wanted to kill Titlacauan and destroy the figurine. The people picked up stones and hurled them at the magician. Over and over again they threw stones at him, until finally he fell down, dead, and his body was left there to rot.

It did not take long before the corpse began to stink. The odor was more horrendous than any the people had encountered before. But not only that: those who smelled the stink of the magician's corpse were killed, and when the wind carried the stench about the land, the people died who smelled it.

But Titlacauan was not yet finished with his mischief, for still he purposed to destroy the Toltecs. And so, he took upon himself a new form and went to Tula, where he said to the people, "Why do you let such a noisome thing sit in your marketplace? Surely it should be removed."

The Toltecs listened to the words of Titlacauan and said, "Yes, this man is quite correct. We should not let this thing stay in our marketplace. Let us get ropes and tie its feet and drag it out of the city."

And so, the men of Tula went and fetched ropes, and they made them fast about the corpse. Then they pulled on the ropes to drag the dead thing away. But the corpse was too heavy; no matter how they pulled, the body would not move. The men of Tula called for aid. They called for others to come and help them pull, and when a great multitude had gathered and taken hold of the ropes, the order was given for all to pull. But still the corpse did not move. Instead, the ropes binding it broke, and the men tumbled down on top of each other, and many were killed in the press of bodies.

Titlacauan went to the men of Tula and said, "Oh, I see that you are not strong enough to pull away a simple corpse. Perhaps you should use my magic song. You should sing, 'Drag, drag, drag away this dead log! Drag him away! Help us drag him, O sorcerer Titlacauan!'"

The men of Tula listened to the song of the magician. They put new ropes about the corpse and began to pull, singing the song the sorcerer taught them. They pulled and pulled, and again the ropes broke, and again many were killed in the tumbling press of bodies.

Over and over this happened. The men would try to pull away the corpse, and many would die when the ropes snapped. But yet they would go back and try again, for they had been ensorcelled by Titlacauan, who wanted them to destroy their selves.

64

A last sorcery that Titlacauan practiced on the Toltecs he did in the guise of an old woman. First, he made it so that the food of the Toltecs went bad. It tasted so bitter that none could bear to eat it. No matter what food was prepared, or how it was prepared, it was unfit to eat. And so, the Toltecs became very hungry, and the other peoples in the lands laughed at them.

After taking on the guise of an old woman, Titlacauan went to Xochitlan (Place of the Flower), where there were gardens floating upon the water as well as gardens of many flowers upon the land. There Titlacauan sat in his guise as an old woman, toasting maize. The aroma of toasting maize floated up from her cookfire. It wafted away on the wind. It went along the fields and over the hills. It went into the temples and into the houses of the people. And everywhere the Toltecs said, "What is this aroma of toasting maize? Where does it come from? Surely now we shall have good food to eat, if we can find who is toasting this maize."

And so, the Toltecs set out in great numbers to find where this good maize was. They left their homes in Tula and went to Xochitlan, and they arrived quickly, for the Toltecs had the gift of moving from place to place very swiftly.

When the Toltecs arrived at the place where Titlacauan was, the sorcerer took up a great sword and slew them all as they came. Titlacauan cut them down one after another in his guise of an old woman. And so, the peoples of the lands around made sport of the Toltecs, for the old woman had slain so many of them.

Huemac Plays the Ball Game

An important early modern source of Aztec myths is the now-missing Codex Chimalpopoca, *a manuscript written in 1558 in Nahuatl and Spanish. The telling of the "Legend of the Suns" in this codex contains a story about Huemac, the mythical last king of the Toltecs, who learns a hard lesson about courtesy and the honor due to divine beings. As with the stories about Huemac from the contemporary*

Florentine Codex, *this tale was created in an attempt to legitimize Aztec rule.*

In this section of the legend, Huemac plays tlachtli, *the sacred ball game, with the* tlaloque, *servants of the rain-god, Tlaloc. Tlachtli was played by many Mesoamerican cultures. The rules required players to use only their hips and knees to strike a solid rubber ball that was about six inches in diameter. Because of the heavy ball and the rough play of the game, athletes wore protective gear made out of deerskin. Although there is some variation in the size and shape of extant courts, playing spaces often were in the shape of a capital letter "I" flanked by stone walls. At the midpoint of the walls on the long sides of these courts were stone hoops with barely enough space for the ball to pass through. Hitting the ball through the hoop ended the game, and the team who had scored that goal was the winner. However, these goals were rare, and there were other means of keeping score in order to determine who won or lost.*

In this story, Huemac and his opponents wager jade and quetzal feathers on the outcome of their game. Mesoamerican cultures used feathers of the quetzal and other birds as an important agricultural product and trade item. Quetzal feathers, especially, were prized for their beauty and brilliant colors, but not just anyone could wear these; they were a symbol of nobility and power, and as such were given as prizes to the bravest warriors, or were worn as tokens of authority by the king and holders of government office.

One day, Huemac, king of the Toltecs, was of a mind to play the ball game. He thought about whom he might invite to play with him, but could think of no one who would give him a true challenge, for Huemac was the best player of tlachtli that had ever lived. And so, the king was vexed and invited no one, and he walked about in a sour mood grumbling to himself. Word came to the tlaloque, the lords of rain who serve Tlaloc, the god of rain, that Huemac wanted to play tlachtli but could find no one good enough to face him, so the tlaloque went to Tula and said that they would play with Huemac.

Huemac was delighted by this, for here surely were players who would present a challenge to his skills.

The tlaloque asked Huemac, "Shall we have a wager on our game?"

Huemac answered, "Yes, indeed we shall! I wager my jade and my quetzal feathers."

The tlaloque said, "It is well. We also wager our jade and quetzal feathers."

Then the tlaloque and Huemac went down to the ball court and they played the game. No matter how swiftly the tlaloque ran, no matter how hard they hit the ball with their hips and knees, they were no match for the skill of Huemac. Finally, the king gave the ball a mighty stroke, it went through the hoop at the side of the court, and the tlaloque had to admit defeat.

The tlaloque brought their wager to Huemac. They gave him ears of maize in their green husks, for this to them was jade and quetzal plumes. But Huemac was insulted by this, for he had expected precious stones and bright feathers. "What is this?" said Huemac. "This is not precious jade, nor beautiful quetzal feathers. It is only maize. Take it away!"

And so, the tlaloque took away the maize and gave to Huemac jade as a precious stone and quetzal plumes as bright feathers, and when this was done, they said to the king, "Because of your insolence and greed, we will take away our own jade from you and your people. We will keep it from you and the people for four years."

Soon Huemac learned the great cost of his rudeness. The tlaloque made a great storm of hail fall on the land of the Toltecs. The hail fell out of the sky in a great shower, and when it was done, there was hail up to a man's knee all over the whole land. All the crops were buried and died from the cold and the striking of the hail. Then the sun came out. It came out and it shone mercilessly down on Tula. It shone on the maguey and nopal cacti, the trees, and the grass, drying them all up. The sun shone so much and so hotly that even the stones began to crack from the heat and dryness, for the tlaloque held back the rain as well. And so, it was that the Toltecs could not grow enough food to eat, and many of them died from hunger.

Finally, at the end of the four years, the tlaloque brought back the rain. One day, as it rained, a Toltec man walked along next to a pool of water, and out of the pool rose a ripe ear of corn that someone had already begun to eat. The man plucked the ear out of the water and began to eat it himself. Suddenly, a priest of Tlaloc, the rain-god, also emerged from the pool of water.

"Have you learned your lesson?" said the priest.

"Most assuredly I have, O Holy One," said the man, "and so have all my brothers and sisters."

"That is well," said the priest. "Wait for me here, for I go to speak to the lord of rain."

The priest went back under the water, and when he reappeared his arms were full of ripe ears of maize. "Take these to Huemac," said the priest. "Tell him that if he wishes the rain to come back, he will give the gods the daughter of Tozcuecuex the Mexica, for surely the Mexica will eat the Toltecs just as you eat the maize."

The man did as the priest commanded. When Huemac heard the message of the gods, he wept, for he understood that although the rains would come again, the kingdom of the Toltecs was at an end. Huemac sent messengers to the Mexica to demand the young woman be brought to him. The messengers told the Mexica that the young woman was demanded by the gods. And so, the Mexica prepared for a sacrifice by fasting for four days. And when the time of fasting and preparation was over, they gave the young woman to the gods, sacrificing her in Pantitlan. When the sacrifice was complete, the tlaloque appeared to Tozcuecuex, the father of the girl, saying, "Grieve not for your daughter, for she will be with you."

Then they put the girl's heart and many different kinds of food into Tozcuecuex's tobacco pouch. The tlaloque said to Tozcuecuex,

"Here is food for the Mexica. Be of good courage, for surely the Toltecs will be destroyed and the Mexica will inherit their lands."

When this was done, the tlaloque brought much rain. It rained for four days and four nights, and when it was done raining, the grass, trees, and crops all began to sprout and grow, and soon there was enough food for all to eat. But in the end, what the gods had said came true: the Toltecs were destroyed. Huemac ran away to hide in a cave, and his people were scattered to many other places, and the Mexica came to rule over those lands.

How Quetzalcoatl Became the Morning Star

As with the legend of Huitzilopochtli and the migration of the Mexica, the story of Quetzalcoatl's departure from Tula, the Toltec capital, may be based in part on historical events, although it is extremely difficult to untangle facts from the web of myth. The ancient Toltec civilization in Tula gave the title "Quetzalcoatl" to their priest-kings, and at its height, the Toltec civilization appears to have been one of peace and plenty, with many fine temples. In the legend retold below, it is the Aztec god of the Smoking Mirror who tricks the Toltec Quetzalcoatl into a series of indiscretions that lead to Quetzalcoatl abandoning Tula. Like the stories of Huemac and the sorcerers, presented above, this tale also comes from the Florentine Codex.

There was a time when the god Quetzalcoatl lived upon the earth, and he was lord of Tula, the city of the Toltecs. Quetzalcoatl ruled wisely and well, and the city of Tula was a wealthy place with many palaces full of riches. The fields were always full of grain and vegetables. The markets were always busy with trade. No one in Tula ever wanted for anything.

As priest-king of Tula, Quetzalcoatl was always mindful of the things he must do. He made offerings in their seasons. He pricked his body with thorns to give blood to the gods. Nightly he prayed and went to bathe in the great river that flowed through the city.

Quetzalcoatl did these things faithfully for a long time, and so Tula prospered.

Tezcatlipoca looked upon Tula and became very jealous of her good fortune. Also, Tezcatlipoca had not forgiven Quetzalcoatl the insult of having knocked him out of the sky when he was the First Sun. And so, the god of the Smoking Mirror thought how he might bring about the downfall of his brother, the Plumed Serpent. Tezcatlipoca therefore disguised himself as a young man. He brewed some pulque and put it in a jar. He wrapped the jar and his obsidian mirror in a rabbit skin and set out for Tula. When he arrived at Quetzalcoatl's palace, Tezcatlipoca walked up to his brother's servants and said, "Tell your lord that I am here to show him himself."

The servants showed Tezcatlipoca into Quetzalcoatl's palace. Still disguised as a young man, Tezcatlipoca said, "My lord, I can show you a good and rare thing. I can show you to yourself as you truly are. Very few have this knowledge. I think you should be one of them, for you are lord of a mighty city, and it is right that you should know yourself."

Quetzalcoatl said, "You may do this thing. Show to me myself."

Tezcatlipoca held up his obsidian mirror. Quetzalcoatl gazed into it. And in the mirror he saw a very old man. His hair and beard were white. His skin was wrinkled and his hands all gnarled. "Oh!" cried Quetzalcoatl. "I am so very old and ugly! How will my people see me? How will they stand to look at me? I must hide myself away and never show my face again."

"Never fear, my lord," said Tezcatlipoca. "I have here a medicine that will restore to you your youth."

Tezcatlipoca offered the jar of pulque to Quetzalcoatl. "No, I must not drink that," said Quetzalcoatl. "I am ill."

The god of the Smoking Mirror said, "Nonsense. Drink just a little taste of it. You will see how it aids you."

Over and over Quetzalcoatl refused the pulque. And over and over Tezcatlipoca urged him to drink it. Finally, Quetzalcoatl gave in. He took one sip of the pulque. It was delicious! He had never had anything quite like it. He drank the whole jar, and soon he was very drunk.

Quetzalcoatl sent for his sister, Quetzalpetlatl. He wanted her to drink pulque with him. Quetzalpetlatl came to Tula and went to her brother's palace. There she also drank much pulque, and soon she was as drunk as her brother. That night, Quetzalcoatl was so drunk he forgot to make offerings and say prayers. He forgot to bathe in the great river as a priest-king of Tula ought to do. He spent the night singing and drinking with his sister, and when they both became too weary to do anything more, they went to Quetzalcoatl's chamber where they lay together in his bed until the sun was high in the sky the next day.

When Quetzalcoatl awoke and saw his sister sleeping next to him, he recalled what he had done the night before and felt greatly ashamed. He knew that he could no longer be the king of Tula with so many sins on his soul. Quetzalcoatl decided that he must perform a penance and then leave his beloved city forever. First, he ordered his artisans to make him a fine tomb. When this was done, Quetzalcoatl had himself sealed in the tomb. He remained there for four days. After the four days were over, Quetzalcoatl came out of his tomb. He burned down his fine palace. He buried his gold and his jewels. The beautiful birds who gave him their bright feathers he sent away. The cacao trees he transformed into lowly mesquites. And when all this was done, Quetzalcoatl walked out of Tula, weeping all the while at the loss of his beautiful city.

Quetzalcoatl walked ever eastward, away from the beautiful city of Tula. After a time, he came upon a tree in a place called Quauhtitlan, the Place of the Tree. The tree was very old and gnarled. Quetzalcoatl gazed upon the tree and remembered what he had seen in Tezcatlipoca's mirror. "We are very old, you and I," he said to the tree, and from that time forth that place was known as

Huehuequauhtitlan, the Place of the Old Tree. Before leaving that place, Quetzalcoatl picked up many stones and hurled them at the tree. He threw them with such force that they went deep into the tree's bark, and there they remained.

The Plumed Serpent resumed his journey. Ever eastward he went, away from his beautiful city. He walked until he was very weary. Quetzalcoatl looked about him for a place to rest. Nearby there was a great stone. Quetzalcoatl rested himself on the stone, leaning on it with his hands. While he rested, he looked back towards his beautiful city, and once more he began to weep. The god's tears rolled down his face and splashed onto the rock. Soon his tears had made holes in the surface of the rock, and when the god took his hands away, the prints of his hands also were there in the stone. Ever afterward that place was called Temalpalco, the Place Marked by Hands.

Once more, Quetzalcoatl resumed his journey. He walked ever eastward until he came to a place where there was a great river. Quetzalcoatl wanted to cross the river, but there was no bridge. So, the god took many great stones and made for himself a bridge, and thus he crossed the river. And so, the place afterward became known as Tepanoayan, the Place of the Stone Bridge.

Next Quetzalcoatl came to a place where there were many sorcerers. The sorcerers came to the god and asked, "Where are you going?"

Quetzalcoatl said, "I am going east, to Tlapallan."

"Why are you going there?" asked the sorcerers.

"I go because I must," said Quetzalcoatl. "The sun calls me thither."

"Before you leave," said the sorcerers, "teach to us the crafts of metalworking and jewelsmithing. Teach us the crafts of building and of weaving with feathers, for we know that you are learned in these arts."

Quetzalcoatl did not want to part with this knowledge, but the sorcerers forced him to teach them. When Quetzalcoatl had taught them all he knew, he took a fine necklace that he was wearing and threw it into the fountain that was nearby. Thus, that place became known as Cozcaapan, the Place of Jeweled Waters.

Quetzalcoatl left Cozcaapan, walking ever eastwards. As he walked down the road, he was met by another sorcerer. "Where are you going?" asked the sorcerer.

"I am going east, to Tlapallan," said Quetzalcoatl.

"That is a good journey to make," said the sorcerer, "but you may not leave this place until you have had a drink of pulque."

Quetzalcoatl remembered his shame that came from drinking pulque. He said to the sorcerer, "I must not taste of that drink."

"Be that as it may," said the sorcerer, "I will not let you continue your journey until you have tasted of the pulque."

Quetzalcoatl saw that he had no choice. He drank the pulque the sorcerer gave him, and soon he became drunk. He lay down and fell fast asleep and began to snore. And his snores were so loud that they were heard far away, and the people far away thought to themselves, "Ah, it is thunder."

After a time, Quetzalcoatl awoke from his slumber. He looked about him and remembered where he was and what he must do. He straightened his hair and neatened his clothing. Before he resumed his journey, he named that place Cochtocan, the City of Sleepers.

On and on Quetzalcoatl traveled, until he climbed into the high mountain pass between Popocatepetl, the Smoking Mountain, and Iztac tepetl, the White Mountain. There it began to snow. White flurries came down from the sky, and the wind grew chill. There was much ice on the path. It was so cold that the servants who had come with Quetzalcoatl died of it, and the god mourned them very greatly. And when the god was done singing laments for his servants, he traveled on through the mountains. It is said that when he needed to descend a mountain, he would rest himself by sitting on the snow and ice and sliding to the bottom.

Wherever Quetzalcoatl went, he did some deed for the people of the villages and towns he passed through. In some places, he built ball courts. In others, he planted maguey cactus. Quetzalcoatl did many wonders and many useful things on his journey, and he gave names to all the places he went.

Finally, Quetzalcoatl came to the shore of the sea. And no one knows exactly what happened to him there, for there are two tales told of the fate of the Plumed Serpent. One tale says that he built himself a raft of serpents and sailed away into the east, to Tlapallan, the Red Land, and those who believe this story say that someday Quetzalcoatl will return.

The other tale says that when he arrived at the shore of the sea, he gathered much wood and kindled a huge bonfire. When the fire was big and hot enough, Quetzalcoatl threw himself upon it. In the fire, his body was transformed, and he rose into the sky where he became the Morning Star. And those who believe this tale say that ever since then Quetzalcoatl has acted as herald to the sun, leading it into the sky at each new day.

Glossary

Translations of Nahuatl names given when available.

Name	Literal Meaning	Function
Aztec	"People from Aztlan"	Peoples who lived in Central Mexico and established an empire there
Aztlan	"Place of the White Heron"	Mythical place of origin of the Aztecs
Cacatepec/Cacatepeca		Mythical enemies of the Toltecs
Centzon Huitznahua	"Four Hundred Southerners"	Sons of Coatlicue who represent the stars
Chalchiuhtlicue	"Jade Skirt Woman"	Goddess of waterways; wife of Tlaloc
Chapultepec	"Hill of the Locusts"	Ancient Toltec city on the shores of Lake Texcoco

Chichimecs		General term for non-Aztec peoples; often has connotations of barbarism
Cihuacoatl	"Woman Serpent"	Goddess of midwifery
Cipactli		Giant fish whose body was turned into the earth by Quetzalcoatl and Huitzilopochtli
Cipactonal		First man (or woman)
Coatepec	"Serpent Mountain"	Home of Coatlicue
Coatepec/Coatepeca	"Hill of Snakes"/ "People of the Hill of Snakes"	Mythical enemies of the Toltecs
Coatlicue	"Serpent-Skirt"	Mother of the moon, stars, and Huitzilopochtli
Cochtocan	"City of Sleepers"	Place in Quetzalcoatl's journey from Tula
Copil		Son of Malinalxochitl and enemy of Huitzilopochtli and the Mexica
Coyolxauhqui	"Precious Bells"	Daughter of Coatlicue whose head becomes the moon
Cozcaapan	"Place of Jeweled Waters"	Place in Quetzalcoatl's journey from Tula

Culhuacan		Ancient Toltec city
Ehecatl	"Wind"	Aspect of Quetzalcoatl as god of wind
Huehuequauhtitlan	"Place of the Old Tree"	Place in Quetzalcoatl's journey from Tula
Huemac		Mythical last king of the Toltecs
Huitzilopochtli	"Hummingbird of the Left" or "Hummingbird of the South"	God of war
Itztlacoliuhqui	"Curved Obsidian"	God of cold and obsidian; transformed aspect of Tlahuizcalpantecuhtli
Ixtapalapan		Place along the shore of Lake Texcoco where the Mexica settle as part of their journey
Ixnextli	"Ashen Eyes"	Transformation of Xochiquetzal when she is exiled from Tamoanchan
Iztac tepetl	"White Mountain"	Mountain in the Valley of Mexico
Lake Texcoco		Ancient lake in Central Mexico; now the site of Mexico City
Macehuales		Aztec farmers;

commoners

Malinalco		Mythical city founded by Malinalxochitl
Malinalxochitl	"Wild Grass Flower"	Daughter of Coatlicue and enemy of Huitzilopochtli and the Aztecs
Mayahuel		Goddess of the maguey cactus
Mexica		One of the tribes of Aztlan who migrated to Central Mexico
Michoacán		Region of Mexico; stopping-place of the Mexica on their journey south
Mictecacihuatl	"Lady of Mictlan"	Consort of Mictlantecuhtli
Mictlan		Land of the dead
Mictlantecuhtli	"Lord of Mictlan"	God of the dead
Mixcoatl	"Cloud Serpent"	God of hunting and the Milky Way; inventor of blood offerings and ritual warfare
Nahuatl		Language spoken by the Aztecs
Nanahuatzin	"Full of Sores"	God of disease; sacrifices self and is transformed into the

		Fifth Sun
Ollin Tonatiuh/Tonatiuh	"Movement of the Sun"	God of the sun; transformed aspect of Nanahuatzin
Ometeotl	"Dual God" or "God of Duality"	Main creator-god
Oxomoco		First man (or woman)
Pantitlan		Mythical place where the daughter of the Mexica king is sacrificed in the legends about Huemac
Patzcuaro		Stopping-place of the Mexica on their journey south
Piltzintecuhtli		Son of Oxomoco and Cipactonal
Popocatepetl	"Smoking Mountain"	Volcano in the Valley of Mexico
Quauhtitlan	"Place of the Tree"	Place in Quetzalcoatl's journey from Tula
Quetzalcoatl	"Plumed Serpent"	God of knowledge, crafts, and the Morning Star
Quetzalpetlatl		Sister of Quetzalcoatl
Tamoanchan	"Land of the Misty Sky"	Mythical paradise where the gods live and human beings are remade under the Fifth Sun

Tecuciztecatl	"The One from the Place of the Conch"	God of the moon
Temalpalco	"Place Marked by Hands"	Place in Quetzalcoatl's journey from Tula
Tenochtitlan	"Place of the Nopal Cactus"	Ancient city on the waters of Lake Texcoco; capital city and ritual center of the Aztec Empire
Teotihuacan	"Place of the Road of the Gods"	Ancient Aztec city and ritual center
Tepanoayan	"Place of the Stone Bridge"	Place in Quetzalcoatl's journey from Tula
Texcalpan		Place mentioned in the stories of Titlacauan and Huemac
Tezcatlipoca	"Smoking Mirror"	God of night, enmity, and strife
Titlacauan	"We Are His Slaves"	Aspect of Tezcatlipoca; appears as a sorcerer in stories about Huemac and the fall of the Toltecs
Tizapan		Place given to the Mexica by the king of Culhuacan
Tlahuizcalpantecuhtli	"Lord of Dawn"	God of the Morning Star

Tlaloc	"He Who Makes Things Sprout"	God of rain; husband of Xochiquetzal
Tlaloque		Servants of Tlaloc; associated with rain, thunder, lightning, and hail
Tlaltecuhtli	"Earth Lord"	Monster from whose body Quetzalcoatl and Tezcatlipoca remake the heavens and the earth
Tlapallan	"Red Land"	Legendary place that was the goal of Quetzalcoatl's journey from Tula
Tlachtli		Mesoamerican sacred ball game
Toltecs	"People of Tula"	Ancient civilization in Central Mexico that was replaced by the Aztecs
Tonacacihuatl	"Lady of Our Sustenance"	Female aspect of Ometeotl; consort of Tonacacihuatl
Tonacatecuhtli	"Lord of Our Sustenance"	Male aspect of Ometeotl; consort of Tonacacihuatl
Tonacatepetl	"Mountain of Food"	Mythical mountain in which Quetzalcoatl finds maize and other foodstuffs

Tozcuecuex		Mythical king of the Mexica in legends about Huemac
Tula	"Place of the Rushes"	Capital city of the Toltec Empire
Tzatzitepetl	"Mountain That Speaks"	Mythical mountain outside of the Toltec capital
Tzitzimitl (pl. tzitzimime)		Goddess(es) of the stars
Xipe Totec	"Flayed God"	God of agriculture, growing plants, and seasons
Xochimilco	"People of the Flower Field"	Nahuatl-speaking tribe who migrated into Central Mexico
Xochiquetzal	"Flower Quetzal Feather"	Goddess of fertility, beauty, and young mothers; wife of Tlaloc
Xochitlan	"Place of the Flower"	Toltec garden city

Check out more mythology books by Matt Clayton

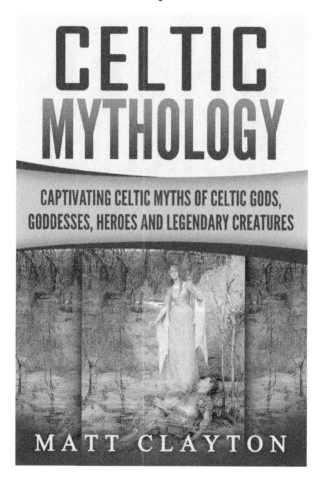

GREEK
MYTHOLOGY

A CAPTIVATING INTRODUCTION TO GREEK MYTHS OF GREEK GODS, GODDESSES, HEROES, AND MONSTERS

MATT CLAYTON

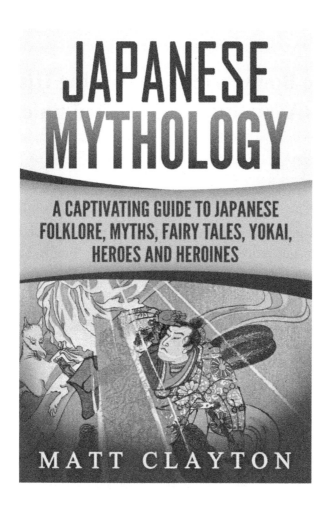

JAPANESE MYTHOLOGY

A CAPTIVATING GUIDE TO JAPANESE FOLKLORE, MYTHS, FAIRY TALES, YOKAI, HEROES AND HEROINES

MATT CLAYTON

Free Bonus from Captivating History (Available for a Limited time)

Hi History Lovers!

Now you have a chance to join our exclusive history list so you can get your first history ebook for free as well as discounts and a potential to get more history books for free! Simply visit the link below to join.

Captivatinghistory.com/ebook

Also, make sure to follow us on:

Twitter: @Captivhistory

Facebook: Captivating History:@captivatinghistory

Bibliography

Alexander, Harley Burr. *Mythology of All Races*. Vol. 11, *Latin-American*. Boston: Marshall Jones Co., 1920.

Allan, Tony, and Tom Lowenstein. *Gods of Sun & Sacrifice: Aztec & Maya Myth*. London: Duncan Baird Publishers, 1997.

Bancroft, Hubert Howe. *The Native Races of the Pacific States of North America*. Vol. 3, *Myths and Languages*. San Francisco: A. L. Bancroft Co., 1875.

Bierhorst, John, trans. *History and Mythology of the Aztecs: The Codex Chimalpopoca*. Tucson: University of Arizona Press, 1992.

Brinton, Daniel G. *American Hero-Myths: A Study in the Native Religions of the Western Continent*. Philadelphia: H. C. Watts & Co., 1882.

Burland, Cottie Arthur, et al. *Mythology of the Americas*. London: Hamlyn Publishing Group, 1970.

Carrasco, David. *The Aztecs: A Very Short Introduction*. Oxford: Oxford University Press, 2012.

Clendennin, Inga. *Aztecs: An Interpretation*. Cambridge: Cambridge University Press, 1991.

Coe, Sophie D. *The True History of Chocolate.* London: Thames and Hudson, Ltd., 1996.

Dalal, Anita. *Myths of Pre-Columbian America.* Austin: Steck-Vaughn Company, 2001.

Durán, Diego. *Historia de las Indias de Nueva España y Islas de Tierra Ferme.* Ed. José F. Ramirez. Vol. 1. México: J. M. Andrade y F. Escalante, 1867.

Faiella, Graham. *Mesoamerican Mythology.* New York: The Rosen Publishing Group, Inc., 2006.

Ferguson, Diana. *Tales of the Plumed Serpent: Aztec, Inca and Mayan Myths.* London: Collins & Brown, Ltd., 2000.

Hunt, Norman Bancroft. *Gods and Myths of the Aztecs.* London: Brockhampton Press, 1996.

Jonghe, Édouard de, ed. "Histoyre du Mechique: Manuscrit français inédit du XVIe siècle." *Journal de la société des américanistes* 2 (1905): 1-41.

Léon-Portilla, Miguel, ed. *Native Mesoamerican Spirituality: Ancient Myths, Discourses, Stories, Doctrines, Hymns, Poems from the Aztec, Yucatec, Quiche-Maya, and Other Sacred Traditions.* Mahwah: Paulist Press, 1980.

————. Trans. Jack Emory Davis. *Aztec Thought and Culture: A Study of the Ancient Nahuatl Mind.* Norman: University of Oklahoma Press, 1963.

Markman, Roberta H. and Peter T. Markman. *The Flayed God: The Mesoamerican Mythological Tradition.* New York: Harper Collins Publishers, 1992.

McDermott, Gerald. *Musicians of the Sun.* New York: Simon & Schuster, 1997.

Mendieta, Gerónimo de. *Historia eclesiástica indiana.* Joaquin Garcia Icazbalceta, ed. n.c.: F. Diaz de Leon y S. White, 1870.

Miller, Mary, and Karl Taube. *An Illustrated Dictionary of the Gods and Symbols of Ancient Mexico and the Maya*. London: Thames & Hudson, Ltd, 1993.

Nardo, Don. *Aztec Mythology*. Farmington Hills: Lucent Books, 2015.

Phillips, Henry. "Notes Upon the *Codex Ramirez*, With a Translation of the Same." *Proceedings of the American Philosophical Society* 21 (1883): 616-651.

Radin, Paul. "The Sources and Authenticity of the History of the Ancient Mexicans." *University of California Publications in American Archaeology and Ethnology* 17/1 (1920): 1-150.

Roberts, Timothy R. *Myths of the World: Gods of the Maya, Aztecs, and Incas*. New York: MetroBooks, 1996.

Roy, Cal. *The Serpent and the Sun: Myths of the Mexican World*. New York: Farrar, Straus & Giroux, 1972.

Sahagún, Fray Bernardino de. *The Florentine Codex: General History of the Things of New Spain*. Book 3: *The Origins of the Gods*. Trans. Arthur J. O. Anderson et al. *Monographs of the School of American Research* 14/4. Santa Fe: School of American Research and the University of Utah, 1952.

Schuman, Michael A. *Mayan and Aztec Mythology*. Berkeley Heights: Enslow Publishers, Inc., 2001.

Smith, Michael E. *The Aztecs*. 3rd ed. Chicester: Wiley-Blackwell, 2011.

Torquemada, Juan de. *Primera parte de los veinte i vn libros rituales i monarchia indiana: con el origen y guerras, de los indios ocidentales, de sus poblaçones: descubrimento, conquista, conuersion, y otras cosas marauillosas de la mesma tierra*. Vol. 2. Madrid: Nicolas Rodriquez Franco, 1723.

Taube, Karl. *The Legendary Past: Aztec and Maya Myths*. London: British Museum Press, 1993.